WALKING
through the
VALLEY *of*
TEARS

One Man's Journey from Grief to Gratitude

BUDDY MCELHANNON

WESTBOW·
PRESS
A DIVISION OF THOMAS NELSON
& ZONDERVAN

Unless otherwise noted, Scripture taken from the *New American Standard Bible*®, copyright © 1960, 1962, 1963, 1968, 1971, 1972, 1973, 1975, 1977, 1995 by The Lockman Foundation. Used by permission.

Other Scripture quotations noted as RSV are from *The Revised Standard Version of the Bible*: Catholic Edition, copyright © 1965, 1966 the Division of Christian Education of the National Council of the Churches of Christ in the United States of America. Used by permission. All rights reserved.

WestBow Press books may be ordered through booksellers or by contacting:

WestBow Press
A Division of Thomas Nelson & Zondervan
1663 Liberty Drive
Bloomington, IN 47403
www.westbowpress.com
1 (866) 928-1240

Because of the dynamic nature of the Internet, any web addresses or links contained in this book may have changed since publication and may no longer be valid. The views expressed in this work are solely those of the author and do not necessarily reflect the views of the publisher, and the publisher hereby disclaims any responsibility for them.

Any people depicted in stock imagery provided by Thinkstock are models, and such images are being used for illustrative purposes only. Certain stock imagery © Thinkstock.

ISBN: 978-1-4908-2687-5 (sc)
ISBN: 978-1-4908-2688-2 (hc)
ISBN: 978-1-4908-2686-8 (e)

Library of Congress Control Number: 2014903035

Printed in the United States of America.

WestBow Press rev. date: 03/25/2014

To my children, Joel, Russ, Taryn, Maggie, and Mari, and to each of their spouses. Unless the Lord comes soon, you or your spouse will likely walk through this same valley. May the path I have taken provide encouragement and comfort to you. I love you more than words can say. Know that there is always hope for those who take refuge in the Lord.

Surely he has borne our griefs and carried our sorrows.
—Isaiah 53:4 RSV

I do not understand the mystery of grace—only that it meets
us where we are and does not leave us where it found us.
—Anne Lamott, novelist

Let us then with confidence draw near to the
throne of grace, that we may receive mercy
and find grace to help in time of need.
—Hebrews 4:16 RSV

If I have learned anything during this walk through the valley
of tears, it is that God is near the brokenhearted, His grace is
sufficient, and grief is a battle fought best with a grateful heart.
Thank you, Lord, for Your grace and mercy endures forever.
—Buddy McElhannon, February 2012

Introduction

When my wife, Tootie, and I sat in our living room in October 2010 and decided to be open about her battle with cancer, we had no idea where that would lead or how short a journey it would be. We started using the mylifeline.org website to keep friends and family updated about her progress. We soon discovered that our willingness to be transparent provided a window for so many others to do more than just watch, to actually participate in a remarkable spiritual journey. Tootie's gallant fight ended January 28, 2011. Mine, I soon discovered, had only begun.

As my period of grief began, I decided to continue writing about my walk through this valley of tears. Journaling this walk proved to be as helpful for me as writing the blog had been during Tootie's battle with cancer. And, as we learned with the blog, I have decided that transparency can be a good and blessed thing. At the risk of an occasional "too much information" moment, I have endeavored to be open and honest about my journey of grief and, more importantly, how the Lord has been my comfort, my Redeemer, and my friend.

I first feared that anyone reading my rambling notes and reflections would only feel pity for this grieving soul. So I asked a good friend, who is a psychologist, to read my first three months of notes. "Am I going nuts?" I asked. After reading it, he smiled and calmed my fears by observing, "No, you are normal!" He thanked me and shared that he and his wife had read my journal. Both had been touched and encouraged, as they themselves were going through a period of grief with a parent. Encouraged, I decided to continue documenting my journey for one year.

This first year without my beloved is over. It occurs to me that walking through this personal valley of tears became more than just a stumbling walk through an emotional minefield. This journey was a battle for my soul. Would I succumb to despair, or would I cling to the Rock of Ages? Would I drown in a sea of memories, or would I learn how to cherish them as a reminder of God's blessings and faithfulness?

I soon discovered I was but a frayed rope in a spiritual tug-of-war, with the spirit of despair pulling from one end and the spirit of gratefulness tugging in the opposite direction. I thank God that as I walked and crawled through this valley of tears, I discovered the truth declared in Psalm 34, verses 17 and 18: "The righteous cry, and the LORD hears and delivers them out of all of their troubles. The LORD is near to the brokenhearted and saves those who are crushed in spirit."

Thank you, Lord, for Your comfort of this broken heart.

Walking through the Valley of Tears

February 4, 2011: Disoriented

It wasn't supposed to be this way. This wasn't supposed to happen. Either we would live a long life together or I would die first. I never even considered that Tootie could die at age fifty-nine and leave me alone. Grief hurts, but I never realized how disorienting it would be. Now what do I do? I've never had any plans that did not involve Tootie—none. I am like a lost puppy who doesn't know which way to turn. I just don't know how to make new plans without her.

One day at a time. No, one step at a time. That's all I can do for now. *Show me the way, Lord, one step at a time.*

> Thy word is a lamp to my feet and a light to my path.
> —Psalm 119:105

February 6, 2011: Here Comes the Rain

A cold Sunday finds me returning to the cemetery for the first time—*alone.* I wanted to do this quietly and privately. Silence can be painful; it can also be calming. Today I needed this solitary ride to ponder, remember, and grieve. It's a forty-minute drive from the house, with plenty of time to do all of the above.

On the way home, I had the idea that someone could make a million dollars if he or she could invent windshield wipers for your eyes. It sure would make driving easier. I played a CD we had in Tootie's Highlander. It's one of those country music CDs with all-time favorites. The chorus of one of the songs, "Here Comes the Rain" by the Mavericks, perfectly captured the mood of the day and the condition of my heart:

> Here comes the rain, falling down on me.
> I'm showered in pain.
> Nothing remains of what used to be.

No wonder country songs are so popular. They really do pierce the heart. Is this what grieving feels like?

> I am weary with my sighing; every night I make
> my bed swim, I dissolve my couch with my tears.
> My eye has wasted away with grief ... the Lord has
> heard the voice of my weeping. The Lord has heard
> my supplication, the Lord receives my prayer.
> —Psalm 6:6–7a, 8b, 9

February 8, 2011: The Hardest Question to Answer

Going through the loss of someone close, like a spouse, is difficult on many fronts. I really do understand why some people choose to do this privately. It is so hard to respond to the volume of calls and questions you receive: How are you doing? What can we do to help? I am sorry for your loss.

I have heard those three comments hundreds of times in the past couple of weeks. Of course, each question was asked with sincerity and was received humbly. After all, these are people who care about Tootie and her family. The more questions asked, the greater the love communicated. I was still thankful for each one of them.

Two weeks have passed since Tootie's death, and I have taken some time off to recuperate. I needed this more than I'd thought I would. After running some errands, I entered a local restaurant to grab a bowl of hot soup on this cold, windy day. The hostess approached, and, despite the obvious, she asked, "How many are in your party?"

"Just one," I answered. It's the first time I have said it. It won't be the last. *Just one.* Now that is a lonely number.

Oh, Lord, help me remember that though I may be just one, I am never alone.

Even though I walk through the valley of the
shadow of death, I fear no evil, for Thou art with
me; Thy rod and Thy staff, they comfort me.
—Psalm 23:4

February 10, 2011: Second Thoughts

I'm not sure I expected this. The more I think about it, the more I think that maybe I should have. During the quiet times, my mind is preoccupied with questions. *What else could I have done? Were there signs we missed? Did I spend enough time with her in her final days? Did I tell her often enough how much I loved her?* These second thoughts come over me like a wave of regret.

Ironically, I know she worried about me. Even before the cancer, her chronic back pain greatly impacted how we lived. She apologized for not being able to do some things we normally would have done. Trips were canceled, dinners never planned—all because it was impossible to plan ahead and know how well she would be on any given day.

In her last four months after we discovered the cancer, she spent twenty-nine days in the hospital. When she was at home, she was in bed 80 percent of the time. Yet serving her was never a chore, just another way to express my love for her.

Tootie had her own gift to give. On many days, while lying there in discomfort, she would look at me, and when our eyes met, she would say, as if it was for the very first time, "I love you, Buddy McElhannon." Now, when overwhelmed by those second thoughts, I race to that memory. It is a lifeline, a comfort for me, knowing she knew I was doing all I could. Second thoughts lead me to one memory—the knowledge that we loved till death did us part. No second thoughts about that.

February 11, 2011: Encouragement from Unlikely Sources

One of the missionaries we support financially is Melanie Martin. She serves in Jos, Nigeria. Tensions are growing in Nigeria between Muslims and Christians, but she has refused to leave despite increased risk. In her latest newsletter, she recounted walking into a home where a young son had recently died. The family was singing a classic Christian hymn, "My Jesus, I Love Thee." She quoted the third stanza:

> I'll love Thee in life, I will love Thee in death, And praise Thee as long as Thou lendest me breath;

And say when the death dew lies cold on my brow,
If ever I loved Thee, my Jesus, 'tis now.

I cherish the old hymns. They somehow help me express my deepest feelings. The last line is my prayer, my hope, and my desire: *if ever I loved Thee, my Jesus, 'tis now.*

Amen to that!

February 12, 2011: Applesauce

It's not that I *hate* applesauce; I just do not like it. Now, every time I open the refrigerator door, staring back at me are several single servings of applesauce. During the last two months of Tootie's life, she ate applesauce at least twice a day. It was the easiest way for her to take her pills. She usually took at least five pills in the morning and again in the evening. Swallowing them was an occasional challenge, and she quickly realized it was easier if we placed a pill in the applesauce. Not only did it make it easier to swallow, but it put some food in her stomach.

Applesauce will forever be a reminder of those last few weeks. I or one of our children fed her one spoonful of applesauce with each pill until all the pills and applesauce were gone.

I am surrounded by memories, even applesauce in the fridge. Such memories can either be a constant reminder of what I have lost or something to cherish. Memories are something death can never take away. Feeding her applesauce was an act of love. Maybe that's what I need to remember: applesauce and loving Tootie. I don't like to eat it, but maybe, just maybe, I can savor the memory.

February 14, 2011: Reality Slaps

It's my first day back to work, and the first time in forever that I have not called Tootie at 8:00 a.m. from my office. Such was our daily ritual. I would arrive in the office early, do some work, and then give her a call to see how she was doing and to confirm her plans for the day.

I made no call today, and reality just slapped me in the face. As if the day wasn't hard enough, it is also Valentine's Day, and for the first time in forty-one years I did not buy a card or flowers. No Valentine—yet another slap in the face from reality. The day was not a total loss. Our son Joel and his wife, Rosemary, invited me to Mary Mac's Tea Room for dinner. Good food, great company. Tootie blessed me with five great children and many memories to cherish.

Help me, O Lord, to keep my eyes upon You.
I call upon the Lord, who is worthy to be praised.
—Psalm 18:3

February 15, 2011: Heartbreak

Scripture speaks of marriage as man and woman becoming one flesh (Genesis 2:24). Beyond the obvious physical references, I think that over time a husband and wife become one in many ways. We read each other's thoughts, communicate without even speaking, and pray for each other. How do you become more "one" over time?

Tootie and I could carry on a conversation across a room without saying a word. A raised eyebrow, a slight grin, a nod of the head, and we knew exactly what it meant. I guess there are degrees of oneness. But what happens to spouses when they lose their other half? Heartbreak and heartache. Whom do I wink at now?

Yet those who wait for the Lord will gain new strength; they will mount up with wings like eagles, they will run and not get tired, they will walk and not become weary.
—Isaiah 40:31

February 16, 2011: The Price You Pay

Grief is the price you pay for loving someone. The more you loved, the greater the grief. I have a very high price to pay. The problem is that it is not like some kind of debt you can pay once and for all. No, you cannot prepare for it; it grabs you whenever it chooses. Kleenex is never far away.

The righteous cry, and the Lord hears and delivers them out of all of their troubles. The Lord is near to the brokenhearted and saves those who are crushed in spirit.
—Psalm 34:17–18

February 18, 2011: The Emotional Throttle

I discovered something today. My emotional throttle needs to be tuned up.

A coworker stopped by my office to see how I was doing. Twenty minutes later, I was still talking. Sometimes I start sharing and keep going and going. Later, in another meeting, I found myself becoming agitated with another manager, and realized I came very close to saying the wrong thing in the wrong way. Instead, I grew very quiet and didn't say a word.

I am learning to take a deep breath and wait a minute before responding. Hopefully, time will help me manage these emotions better.

February 19, 2011: Shotgun Saturday

I have yet to feel any real anger. Heartache? Yes. Questions? Yes. Grief? Yes. But I have not been walking around with a baseball bat in my hands, looking for a trash can to hit.

Yet when daughter Maggie invited me to shoot skeet, the idea of shooting something had a strong appeal. Maggie's fiancé Bryan took her and her Peace Corps friends (Nicole and Maggie), who were in town for their annual get-together, to a new gun range near Lake Oconee.

Two hours and fifty shells later, I finished my shooting. Was this good therapy? I don't know, but it felt good to see those orange colored discs explode in midair.

February 22, 2011: Birthday

I turned sixty today. It's my first birthday since 1969 that Tootie isn't around to celebrate. I know she had plans to have a real party, but it was not to be.

However, the kids have again stepped in to fill the breach. Joel took nine of us to Bones Restaurant in Atlanta. We had a private room and talked and laughed for over two and a half hours. I don't recall saying much. I just enjoyed being surrounded by the ones I love the most.

Thank you, Lord, for the blessing of children.

February 24, 2011: Grief Is Exhausting

Grief is exhausting. *Remembering, reflecting,* and *pondering*—all are words that describe mental activities. Why, then, does my body seem so tired afterward? Grief dries up the bones. I have about reached the conclusion that remembering some is okay, but too much for too long is not a good thing.

> Be gracious to me, O LORD, for I am pining away;
> heal me, O LORD, for my bones are dismayed.
> And my soul is greatly dismayed; but Thou, O
> LORD—how long? Return, O LORD, rescue my
> soul; save me because of Thy loving kindness.
> —Psalm 6:2–4

February 25, 2011: Opportunities to Grieve

One of the recent Griefshare.com emails really captured my sense of loss. It reminded me that a spouse represents many different aspects of a person's life, and that each one is an opportunity to experience grief. Amen to that. What aspects should I anticipate grieving? Tootie was

- my companion and best friend;
- my lover;

- my encourager;
- my greatest source of delight;
- my prayer partner;
- the one who shared my private jokes;
- the one who knew me so well;
- the one who managed the house;
- the shoulder on which I cried and the one who cried on my shoulder;
- my cook;
- the arms that embraced and comforted me; and
- my biggest cheerleader—the one I always wanted to make proud.

No wonder the tears flow at every turn. In a weird sort of way, this helps me realize that what I am feeling is normal—painfully normal.

February 26, 2011: I vs. We

Since 1969, I have thought of myself only as *we*, not *I*. Tootie and I started dating in 1969. From that day forward, every thought and action was always *we*-based. Now, for the first time in forty-one years, I have to think as an "I." No wonder I am so dizzy.

February 26, 2011: Birthday Week

Today capped off a rather nice birthday week. The kids were awesome. Tonight (Saturday) we all went bowling. This was followed by a Chinese dinner at Dynasty Restaurant here in Conyers. While my knees, hip, and back are asking me today, "What was I thinking?," it really was a fun time at the bowling alley. And sitting around the dinner table with my brothers and all my children was a joy and comfort.

Tootie would be proud of them.

February 27, 2011: Putting Their Tootie On

One piece of advice I have received is to not be in a hurry to make any key decisions—especially financial ones or ones involving Tootie's personal effects. I consider that good advice. However, with the house being empty during the day, I have a growing concern that it is now a tempting target for thieves. The mere thought of losing Tootie's jewelry, which represents a treasure of precious memories, is more than I can handle. So, as painful as it may be, this is the one thing I wanted to resolve soon.

So, last night after dinner, my three daughters came back to the house, and we spent a few hours going through their mom's jewelry. Looking at a lifetime of Christmas, birthday, and anniversary gifts, one could drown in the memories. More than once I would hear, "I remember when Mom wore this to ..."

Now, to be honest, I did have some concern that the girls would have a tug-of-war over a few items. My concerns proved absolutely unfounded. My daughters were generous, thoughtful, and considerate of each other, even pulling out some items for their two sisters-in-law. I heard more than once, "This looks better on you. Why don't you take this one?"

Today I wrote them a note about last night and said, in part, the following:

> The more I have pondered it, the more I know that I am immensely proud of you, and your mom would be too. I know that wearing your mom's jewelry may bring a tear from time to time.

But what I really want you to think about when you adorn yourself with her jewelry is that your character and the women you are were molded by a mother who loved you unconditionally. You are the living legacy of your mom. The jewelry is just symbolic of it. Whenever you "put your Tootie on," just laugh, knowing that it's been "on" all the time anyway. I love you! When I look upon each of you, I see your mother in so many ways. Thank you for being a living reminder.

Hopefully, as my children have occasion to wear their mother's jewelry, those priceless memories will be something to cherish and spark yet another expression of gratefulness to a God who blessed us with a wonderful wife and mother.

Adorn yourself with eminence and dignity, and
clothe yourself with honor and majesty.
—Job 40:10

February 28, 2011: Love Leaves a Memory that No One Can Steal

Today, I finally wrote a note to my colleagues at AT&T, expressing my gratefulness for their support. It went like this:

Dear Team and AT&T Colleagues,
It's been a month since my wife's funeral and two weeks since I came back to work. It all seems so surreal. Only now does it seem like I can inhale and take a breath. Over the past few months, and especially the last few weeks, I have been

overwhelmed by the compassion and support of family and friends. To say I am grateful is an understatement. It is simply too hard to put into words how blessed I feel for all that I have received from folks like you.

Everyone asks how I am doing. My usual answer is "okay." Forgive me for those brief answers. Some days I really am okay. Other days I feel like our pet Chihuahua, a lost puppy searching the house for my wife. So, some days are good and others are not. I read somewhere that grief is the price you pay for loving someone. So, in a weird sort of way, it's good to know that what I am experiencing is normal. I do have a lot of support, and time will help. Being back at work is good medicine too. I count it a real blessing to be able to work with a group of folks like you.

So thank you for your thoughts, prayers, and acts of kindness. You have been a light during my darkest of days, and I am grateful.

Almost immediately, I got a response from one of my managers: "I really like this old Irish headstone wording: 'Death leaves a heartache no one can heal. Love leaves a memory no one can steal.'"

How true.

Thank you, Lord, that I have great memories to cherish!

March 1, 2011: A Deep Ache

Recently, a friend of a friend, who had followed the website updates about Tootie's walk through the valley of the shadow of death, wrote me the following note: "In some of my reading a couple of days ago, I came across the following, and quite simultaneously, you came to mind: 'The beauty of the soul shines out when a man bears with composure one heavy mischance after another, not because he does not feel them, but because he is a man of high and heroic temper.'"

These are kind words. I must be good at bearing "with composure." I am not sure it is yet an accurate description of me. Time will tell. All I know is that, at this moment, I feel—right down to the marrow in my bones—an ache so deep that I wonder if it will ever go away.

It's strange, but I find it easier to write down my prayers than to verbalize them. At least for now, when I try to pray, the only words that come forth are "Lord, help me." That's it. My heart and soul groan with much more, but for now those three words have become the simplest expression of all the hurt, pain, and heartache.

> Give ear to my prayer, O God; and do not hide Thyself
> from my supplication. Give heed to me, and answer me;
> I am restless in my complaint and am surely distracted,
> —Psalm 55:1–2

March 3, 2011: When Sorrows Like Sea Billows Roll

Today I heard "It Is Well with My Soul" on the radio. This classic hymn is actually the songwriter's response to losing his daughters when they drowned at sea. I had to look up what *billows* meant. It is a "great wave or surge of water." For the first time, I really understand what he meant by "when sorrows like sea billows roll." Oh my, the sorrows sometimes come over me like great waves of grief. Is it well with my soul? I'm not sure I know yet. I'm still too numb.

Oh, Lord, be my lifeboat.

> Hear my cry, O God; give heed to my prayer.
> From the end of the earth I call to Thee when
> my heart is faint; lead me to the rock that is
> higher than I. For Thou hast been a refuge for
> me, a tower of strength against the enemy.
> —Psalm 61:1–3

March 4, 2011: Golf

I played a round of golf yesterday. I had not touched my clubs since last September. These past few months, I have had little time to play golf, much less any desire to play. As much as I love the game, I could not be away from Tootie. It was such a small sacrifice. To be honest, even now I almost have to force myself to play—or do much else. Things take on such a different perspective when you lose half of yourself.

Tom Mitchell, retired AT&T general manager, invited me to play with him at Heron Bay. It turned out that his other partner couldn't play, so it was just the two of us. It was a gorgeous day, and since few others were playing, we took our time and played a leisurely round. I resolved not to talk about Tootie, as I didn't want to dampen the mood, but it wasn't long before Tom asked a few questions. Tom is one of those guys I have known for thirty-plus years, and talking with him came naturally. There seems to be a healing aspect to sharing your burdens within a circle of love and friendship.

It also felt good to get out and do something physical. It proved to be great therapy. Good friends are truly priceless. I even shot an eighty-two, which is normal for me. Not bad after a six-month layoff.

On the 18th hole, I hit a terrible slice off the tee and ended up with a 180-yard blind shot to the green. I pulled out my seven wood, nailed the shot, and knocked it within twenty feet of the pin. As I approached the green, I was smiling and crying at the same time. It felt good to make the shot, but a year ago I would have gone home and shared the story of that shot with Tootie. There was no one to share it with now. Like I said, life takes on a new perspective when you lose your soul mate.

In an email from Griefshare.com (A Season of Grief, Day 4 "*Grief Lasts Longer Than Expected*") I read something Dr. Larry Crabb wrote: "Knowing the Lord and His comfort does not take away the ache; instead, it supports you in the middle of the ache. Until I get home to heaven, there's going to be an ache that won't quit. The grieving process for me is not so much a matter of getting rid of the pain, but not being controlled by the pain."

Amen to that.

Oh, Lord, I'm already weary with my grief, and no end is in sight. Thank you for good friends and a loving family. Help me to find strength and refuge in You, oh Rock of Ages, cleft for me!

March 7, 2011: Prayer by Thomas Merton

I continue to be amazed at the coincidences. I found stuck in my desk at home a business card from someone at church. On the back was a prayer by Thomas Merton. I read it once, twice, and a third time, marveling at how it simply expressed exactly what I am feeling. Coincidence? Hardly.

Thank you, Lord, for standing by the brokenhearted.

This is the prayer from Thomas Merton's book *Thoughts in Solitude*:

> My Lord God, I have no idea where I am going. I do not see the road ahead of me. I cannot know for certain where it will end. Nor do I really know myself, and the fact that I think that I am following your will does not mean that I am actually doing so. But I believe that the desire to please you does in fact please you. And I hope I have that desire in all that I am doing. I hope that I will never do anything apart from that desire. And I know that if I do this you will lead me by the right road though I may know nothing about it. Therefore will I trust you always, though I may seem to be lost and in the shadow of death. I will not fear, for you are ever with me, and you will never leave me to face my perils alone.

March 10, 2011: Lunch with Friends

A couple of retired general managers, Tom Mitchell and Beth Sowell, along with another AT&T employee, Cindy Denman, invited me to join them for lunch today. What a joy! Good friends, good conversation, and good food are a recipe for comfort. We talked, reminisced, laughed, and otherwise enjoyed the pleasure of each other's company. Of course, they inquired about how I was doing, and we spoke about the funeral. Beth's mom is battling cancer, and she was thankful for a copy of the website blog. I continue to be amazed at how Tootie's journey has impacted so many people—and still does.

I find simple joy in the company of family and friends.

March 12, 2011: Silence Is a Megaphone for Grief

Silence is like a burglar alarm that won't turn off. Grief must like silence. At the mere whisper of a cry or the hint of a tear, grief makes its presence known. Silence is a megaphone for grief, a constant, deafening reminder of what I am missing. Yet I find at times that it also promotes a quietness with my Lord. Somehow I need to find a way to cherish the solitude in a positive way.

March 14, 2011: How Am I Doing?

The most common question I am asked is "How are you doing?" I realize that people ask out of concern, but this question, though appreciated, is hard to answer—especially for the thousandth time. Every day is different. I have gotten to the point where I say, "Some days are bad and some not-so-bad."

Some well-meaning folk simply say, "It's going to take some time" or "time heals," as if time itself were the healing agent. I am not so sure about that.

Time alone does take you further from the event, but does it heal you?

I think a person's response to losing a spouse is dynamic, meaning that over time one either stumbles toward despair or slowly allows God to comfort him to the point where the heartache is accepted.

I will never forget my beloved, so how will I ever not have some level of grief? All I know for now is that staying close to the Lord is my only salvation. Psalm 34:18 remains on my lips: "God is near the brokenhearted."

Lord, You and You alone are my salvation. You and You alone can comfort my broken heart, wipe away my tears, and give me hope.

For I, the LORD, am your healer.
—Exodus 15:26

March 16, 2011: Emptiness

I took my first business trip in four months. I arrived in Dallas last Sunday, checked into the hotel, and realized yet again that a habit done a hundred times no longer needed to be repeated: my call home to tell Tootie that I had arrived safely and to give her my contact information.

I no longer needed to make that call.

Usually, when I returned home from such a trip, Tootie greeted me with a long kiss and a hug that promised more to come. When I arrived home today (Wednesday), I found an empty house, an empty bed, and an empty chair at the kitchen table.

Yes, "empty" is an apt description of my life right now. I should stop being surprised by these feelings. They seem to lie in wait and ambush me at the slightest hint of a memory. How is it possible to cherish something that, for now, brings instant pain?

But as for me, I trust in Thee, O LORD,
I say, "Thou art my God." My times are in
Thy hand; deliver me from the hand of my
enemies and from those who persecute me.
—Psalm 31:14–15

March 19, 2011: Staying in the Present

Yesterday was Maggie's birthday, and I took her out to lunch.

Last night I gave Bridget Taylor a call. She is helping me edit the book I am putting together, chronicling Tootie's fight with cancer. The tentative title is *Walking through the Valley of the Shadow.* It's a compilation of the website updates during Tootie's illness and includes great stories that friends have shared. Today (Saturday), daughter Taryn is coming by to hang out with her dad. God bless her. I am just trying to stay in the present while I cherish the memories, which is not easily done.

March 23, 2011: Back Home Again

I went on my second trip in two weeks to Dallas and returned home today. My experience was the same as it was the week before: empty home, empty arms, empty heart.

Grief is indeed that unwelcome companion that fills every void, every moment of silence.

I just keep praying … and crying, but I am still praising the Lord. I'm heartbroken but thankful for His blessings.

Let us therefore draw near with confidence to the
throne of grace, that we may receive mercy and
may find grace to help in our time of need.
—Hebrews 4:16

March 25, 2011: Friday Nights

Friday evenings have become my night to relax. Usually I catch
up on TV shows, watch a movie, and then sleep late on Saturday.

But tonight I started going through a few things. Oh my, we have
so much stuff—too much stuff, actually. I thought I knew where
most of the "stuff" was, but finding certain things like bedsheets,
irons, or teakettles has turned into a treasure hunt. I remember
the quote from financial guru Dave Ramsey: "Debt is bad, saving
is good, giving is fun, and stuff is meaningless."

Never have I agreed more. Stuff is meaningless when compared
to life and souls and faith.

April 2, 2011: Wedding Showers and Good Friends

Daughter Mari and her husband Andrew came into town last
night, for today was a day of showers—wedding showers. Maggie
has two wedding showers today. The first one at 11:00 a.m. is
being held at the home of family friend Patti Willits. A later one
is planned at my sister-in-law Alma's.

Patti has invited all of Tootie's friends, who for years met monthly
to play Pokeno. Tootie had told me that this monthly ritual was
really just a therapy session masquerading as a card game. They

laughed so much that everyone left feeling uplifted. Now these ladies were gathering today to encourage my daughters.

I went to the first shower and helped Dick Willits park the cars. This resulted in my being hugged by fifteen different women. That proved tougher than I expected, as each one offered her condolences and asked how I was doing. I appreciated their compassionate greetings, but I can only take so much of that at one time. Still, it was a generous, loving show of support for Maggie, and it reflected the love that each of these ladies had for Tootie, who was a much-loved woman.

Thank you, Lord, for the blessing of friends and the comfort and grace you pour onto us through their generosity.

April 5, 2011: The Great Malaise

It's Tuesday. It's one of those days when my soul mirrors the weather: dark clouds, no sun, cold, and wet. In other words, it's pretty miserable. How I got up and went to work, I do not know. *Why* I got up and went to work, I do not know. I miss Tootie so much. My heart is in a thousand pieces, and I do not feel like doing anything. I have noticed this kind of malaise just shows up on some days.

> Let my cry come before Thee, O LORD;
> give me understanding according to Thy
> word. Let my supplication come before Thee;
> deliver me according to Thy word.
> —Psalm 119:169–170

April 9, 2011: A Long Day

It's a beautiful Saturday, and my friend Fred Cassidy invited me to the Masters Golf Tournament in Augusta. This place is amazing. Every golf fan should visit at least once. Seeing the best golfers in the world play the best course in the world is a unique experience. The creative skills displayed remind me that we are all made in the image of God.

From Augusta I went to Lake Oconee, where Maggie is having another wedding shower. It was good to meet some of the people that Bryan and his family know. Still, it feels odd to go to any event alone.

Tootie didn't just complete me; she made me feel like we were "more" when we were together than when we were apart. She looked after me, and I looked after her. She helped me evaluate ideas and plans and always seemed to have the right suggestion to make a good idea into a great idea. With her by my side, I always felt confident, secure, and loved. Now, without her encouraging presence, attending a party like this just feels awkward.

April 11, 2011: Into-Me-See

Solitude has its advantages, but they are few. Yes, quiet time can be a good thing—until our dog Cha-Cha barks and barks at the bird she sees through the window. I keep thinking Tootie will walk through the door, returning from a shopping trip. I guess that is a form of denial, but it doesn't last long.

Solitude is the new normal.

I miss her. There is so, so much about her that I miss—and nothing more so than intimacy, real intimacy. I miss the welcome-home kiss, rubbing her feet as we sat on the couch, stroking her hair when her head ached. I miss grabbing her for an impromptu dance in the living room, as we both listened to the music in our hearts. I miss looking into her eyes and knowing what she was thinking ... and her looking into mine and knowing what I was thinking ... and smiling because she was thinking it too.

I heard a speaker once define intimacy as "into-me-see." Such transparency takes a lifetime to develop. Part of the joy of marriage was knowing that there was yet so much to learn about each other. So, yes, I miss the intimacy. It was such a joy to see inside this woman. The depth of her soul had yet to be fully plumbed.

April 13, 2011: Enjoy the Solitude

Living alone is still somewhat surreal. I can understand how easy it is to fall into the trap of isolation. Avoiding the condolences of friends, hiding my emotions, and crying only in private are tempting options. When I am asked a hundred times, "How are you doing?," it is so much easier to say "okay" rather than "not worth a damn."

But I am blessed with good memories, few regrets, a loving family, and a host of caring friends. I'm not sure I could find isolation even if I were looking for it. So I'll just enjoy the solitude between the calls and the invitations.

April 16, 2011: Cherish the Memories

I have an ocean full of memories—good memories, the kind that warm your heart and break it at the same time. I could drown in this sea of forget-me-nots, but I cannot live in the past, of that I am certain. Still, finding balance remains elusive.

When does remembering become an unwillingness to move on? When does the blessing of solitude become the curse of isolation?

Memories are something to cherish, not a land to dwell in forever. Learning how to cherish the memories: that's the challenge. I must be able to pause and grab hold of a favorite memory—like pulling out a favorite picture from an album—recall the joy with great fondness, and then put it back to enjoy again at some future moment.

Be still and know that I am God.
—Psalm 46:10 (RSV)

April 19, 2011: My Response: Worship

The loss of a spouse tests everything about you. Shaken to my core, I have so many questions and so few answers. All I believe is being held up and tested. Do I still believe in God? Now I understand why questions of evil and suffering are the toughest to answer. How easy it is to resent God, to question a God you may no longer even believe in. The first question is a simple one.

Is there a God or not?

Some might view such a personal loss as evidence that no God exists—or if one does, that he is impersonal. I choose to believe in a living, personal God, not out of some sort of wishful thinking, but because I really believe that the evidence is overwhelming—the loss of my wife notwithstanding. We live in a fallen world. Yes, evil, pain, and suffering exist. Yet the God of heaven holds me, binds me, and comforts my broken heart. What else, who else, can I turn to?

I find His healing touch in worship. Man was made to worship. The only question is "What do we worship?" I praise a God who made me, loves me, and comforts me in my grief. Knowing the "Man of Sorrows" helps me to deal with my own.

Thank you, Lord, that the grief I have is something you are intimately familiar with.

Jesus wept.
—John 11:35

April 24, 2011: Easter

This holiday is yet another day to remember all of the Easters that came before. It is so easy to become nostalgic while reflecting on Easter services, Easter egg baskets, and Easter dinners. Yet today was still a day of blessing.

I went to hear my son-in-law Algernon preach at Roswell Street Baptist Church in Marietta. He did a good job. Afterward, he, Taryn, and I met my brothers, Jim and Andy, and my sister-in-law Alma for lunch at Mary Mac's Tea Room in Atlanta. We enjoyed good food and good fellowship.

Later that evening, son Joel and his wife Rosemary dropped by the house, and we ended up having dinner at Waffle House! Yes, it was Easter dinner at Waffle House, but hey, good food is good food, and the company could not have been better.

Later, I realized two things.

One, I am a blessed man. Having a family, as I do, provides a comfort beyond description. The second realization is that I need to give up our dog Cha Cha. Verbalizing my concerns to Joel and Rosemary made me realize that Cha Cha's new normal isn't any more fun than my new normal. She has to spend almost eighteen hours a day in the laundry room during the week. That's not a good life for her. So, I have put the word out that I am looking for a good home for her. This Easter, it turns out, has been eventful, but in an unusual way.

Thank you, Lord, that Your resurrection is a reminder that I have hope and that life has meaning, despite whatever comes my way!

April 29, 2011: Next Up: Maggie's Wedding

How am I going to handle this? In some ways, I am happy beyond words. What father wouldn't be? Tomorrow is my daughter's wedding day. But knowing that Tootie is not here for her and for me is just overwhelming. Tears flow so easily that I have started to keep my pockets full of Kleenex. But I must be strong. I must be thankful for what I had and not allow the sense of loss to rain on Maggie's day. Tootie would be ticked!

April 30, 2011: Wedding Bells …
or Is That a Mandolin?

Wow. The day, the weekend could not have been any better. The weather was perfect. Maggie was absolutely stunning. Her sisters did not let her out of their sight. You would have thought they were joined at the hip. And her new mother-in-law, Libby Combs, stepped in and did so much of what Tootie would have done. She was a blessing.

Yes, the day had its share of tears, tears of joy mixed with tears of heartache over who was not here. Tootie would have been delighted with how it all turned out. The mandolin player who provided the music was a first-class pro. He seemed to strike the right tone and helped foster an atmosphere of reverence and joy.

Lord, even in my darkest moments there is light. Thank you that, while in the midst of grief, I can still rejoice in Maggie and Bryan's marriage!

May 6, 2011: The Ring Comes Off

Soon after the funeral, the thought crossed my mind: *When do I take off my ring?* At the time, my immediate response was "never." I expected the act of removing my wedding band to be a painful act in which I would just relive the whole loss all over again. So, why would I do it? I didn't really expect to marry again, and keeping my ring on seemed like a way to stay connected to Tootie.

But as the days have gone by, and as I have learned more about the grieving process, I have begun to wonder if keeping the ring on is an act of denial. Can I really ever move on if I keep clinging to the past? It is so confusing.

When does cherishing a memory become living in the past?

Well, after a week of golf in Florida with my friend Fred, my hands began to break out in blisters—most likely an allergic reaction to the rubber grips or glue. After all, I had never played golf for four days in a hot environment. My ring irritated the blisters on my left hand, and as I have needed to do in the past, I removed the ring to allow for healing.

Now that my hands have healed, do I put the ring back on? At this point, not having to consciously and deliberately remove it has made it a less painful act. Maybe this was a little grace from God to allow me to remove it without it being such a big deal. I think, for now, I will leave it off. I accept the fact that I am no longer a married man. I need to make this step—a painful step, a tearful step, but one graciously forced upon me. I am not sure this makes any sense to anyone but me, but I am relieved I didn't have to do it consciously.

Lord, thank you for Your love and grace, even in the little things.

May 8, 2011: Mother's Day

I decided to send the kids an email, as they will experience their first Mother's Day without their mom.

> Joel, Russ, Taryn, Maggie, Mari,
>
> This Sunday is one of those occasions when grief seems to shout with a megaphone, as if I have ignored it too long. But it is too hard to ignore. If I have learned anything over the past three months, it is that grief is inevitable, and we should not ignore it. But we can choose how we grieve.
>
> I am not going to tell you how, because each of us must handle it in our own way. I will tell you that I have not ignored it. I have readily admitted to friends and coworkers that some days are not so bad and others are just bad. I have shared my feelings with trustworthy friends and have recognized that I cannot live in the past, but I have admitted that the pain is intense. I

am also choosing to follow your mother's path: she responded to her chronic pain by walking closer with the Lord, and so have I. The only other course is despair, and that is not something that would please your mom, much less the Lord.

The Lord and I have had frequent conversations as of late. I would describe them as part confession, part complaining, part questioning, and part crying—but altogether an appeal for His help. I cannot handle this apart from Him.

I usually end up being thankful for the blessing of your mom. Yes, I miss her beyond anything I can describe. But I also realize that the thirty-eight years of marriage provided me with each of you and countless memories that warm my soul, heart, and mind.

Do I choose bitterness or thankfulness? I have realized that I am always moving in one of those directions. I choose to be thankful. Oh, how blessed a man I am. You are a blessing to me. I hope I can be to you.

Yes, I know Mother's Day will be a hard one. But oh, what a mom you had. So, through the tears, let us still rejoice that Mother's Day is a time of reflection for all of us to remember the mom you had and the wife I had and to be thankful we were so blessed.

Love you all, Dad

May 11, 2011: Filling the Void?

The flip side of enjoying moments of solitude is that the sense of loneliness is, at times, overwhelming. Silence is a constant reminder that Tootie is gone. I find myself even missing some of her favorite TV shows, like *Say Yes to the Dress* or *What Not to Wear*. I can be at a crowded event and *still* feel lonely. Someone is supposed to be hanging on to my arm, but instead I feel like a leg is missing. The loneliness is never greater for me than at night before retiring to bed.

There is no one to kiss good night, no one to read to.

I am beginning to realize that God uses such moments to continue His work within me. My heart aches so much, the temptation is to fill it with worldly things. There is nothing wrong with new relationships, entertainment, or new activities, but if they are used to fill this void or to serve as a distraction, I am falling into a trap. Instead, I am choosing to be more diligent in my devotional life, to seek the Lord and His comfort.

Loneliness is never comfortable, but this very discomfort drives me to the Lord.

Lord, You promise to be near the brokenhearted. I draw near to You so that this period of loneliness is a period of spiritual growth, not despair. Amen.

> We are afflicted in every way, but not crushed;
> perplexed, but not despairing; persecuted, but
> not forsaken; struck down, but not destroyed.
> —2 Corinthians 4:8–9

May 16, 2011: Office with a View

My office is on the 25th floor of the AT&T Tower in downtown Atlanta. It looks east toward Decatur. On the horizon is Stone

Mountain. I find myself taking the occasional mental break, allowing my mind to wander.

Is that a good thing? I don't know.

I find the occasional need to chew on a few memories. It's easy to do on the twenty-fifth floor, looking eastward toward Stone Mountain. That hunk of granite has a mountain of memories.

During our dating years, Tootie and I frequented the state park. Occasionally we'd climb it. More often, we'd find a quiet spot to park and "talk." Usually a lot of "making out" was involved too. I remember that we stayed at the Stone Mountain Inn on the first night of our honeymoon. The following spring, I recall that we had a picnic below the mountain's carving. I still have a picture of a very pregnant Tootie lying on a quilt as we joyfully looked forward to the birth of our first child.

Yes, the memories are as strong and tall as the mountain on the eastern horizon. The mountain isn't going anywhere. Neither are my memories.

May 21, 2011: First Meeting with John Kommeth

Recently I called Maria Kommeth Dunlap to congratulate her on her pregnancy and to inquire about her mother-in-law, Debbie Dunlap, who had lost her husband, Rock, to cancer a few years ago. In talking with Maria, I also asked how her mom, Mary, was doing now, some three years after a car accident that had caused brain trauma. It occurred to me that Maria's dad, John, has suffered a loss of his own. Maybe he would be a good sounding board.

I invited him to breakfast today. We sat and talked for an hour. I think we both appreciated the chance to share with someone whose life had been turned upside down. We decided to make this a Saturday morning ritual, breakfast at 7:00 a.m.

Lord, I am trying to reach out. Thank you for providing these kinds of opportunities to share my grief with someone who understands.

May 28, 2011: Memorial Day Weekend

This weekend proved to be a busy one. Saturday morning, I met John Kommeth again for breakfast. Later, Taryn, Maggie, and Mari came by the house to help clean out Tootie's closet. God bless them. They have no idea how much this means to me.

I brought out a handful of clothes at a time, and they assessed if they wanted to keep an item or give it away. I decided to keep a few select items.

There were just too many memories—like one pair of blue jean cutoff shorts. Oh my, I remember how good she looked in those shorts.

The sight of those legs wound my clock. That memory alone puts a smile on my face. I remember a few times … no, I'd better not go there. I don't know who will read this in the future.

How is it that an old, faded pair of jeans can bring tears and smiles simultaneously?

On Saturday afternoon, I drove out to Buddy and Shug Smith's home to celebrate the high school graduation of their grandchildren, Amber and Austin. Sunday, I met my two sons, Joel and Russ, at their sister Maggie's home. Joel took Russ, his new brother-in-law, Bryan, and me out to a shooting range for a couple of hours. We returned to Maggie and Bryan's home for a cookout. In between, I drove over to Nanny's to visit with everyone. It was the first time I had seen Mom Smith in nine months. I feared that she would ask about Tootie, but she did not. I think her memory is about gone.

May 30, 2011: A Half-Empty Closet

I wasn't prepared for this. The empty closet is yet another trigger point. Yes, I wanted to take the next step and deal with the clothes. But it surprised me how many emotions rose to the surface when I entered the master bedroom closet and saw half of it empty for the first time.

It kind of sums up the condition of my heart.

In such moments as these, darkness and despair come knocking—loudly. Yet I grasp a lifeline once again. From some part of my heart, where seeds of truth have found fertile soil, springs forth a lyric from the opening stanza of the contemporary hymn, "Be Thou Near to Me": "For in my hour of darkness I may be seeking the joy of love unspoken."

When my grief seems the heaviest, my Lord is the nearest. A single lyric from a simple hymn becomes the cry of my heart. *Yes, Lord, be near to me.*

Oh that my vexation were actually weighed and
laid in the balances together with iniquity! For then
it would be heavier than the sand of the seas.
—Job 6:2–3

June 5, 2011: Blessings

During this personal season of mourning, my spirit is sensitive to the words of hymns and songs. A new contemporary song I hear frequently on Christian radio is titled "Blessings," written and sung by Atlanta artist Laura Story.

I cannot listen to this song without thinking of Tootie. The lyrics are so powerful that they prompt me to stop, pray, and ponder God's mercies. The refrain speaks of a spiritual truth that I knew intellectually but learned experientially. This life is not the way it is supposed to be. This is not our final destination, and the world can never satisfy the desires of my heart.

> What if Your blessings come through raindrops?
> What if Your healing comes through tears?
> What if a thousand sleepless nights Are what it
> takes to know You're near?

Oh, Lord, thank you for your mercies in disguise. I may not recognize them, but I know you look beyond the circumstances. Help me to do the same.

June 14, 2011: True Compassion

Many a night I ponder how God's grace flowed to us through family and friends. During Tootie's illness and in the weeks following her death, the outpouring of love and support was nothing short of overwhelming. Cards, calls, and casseroles were a constant reality. I will never forget how a simple expression of love in a card meant so much to us. It was a daily habit for me to read each card to Tootie during those last four months.

I will also remember the countless expressions of sympathy in the weeks following her death. So many folks appreciated the impact Tootie had had on their lives. I will never fail to do the same for friends and family in the future.

As a Christian, Scripture was a comfort on many levels during Tootie's illness. And now, it is even more so. The hymn "Standing on the Promises" comes to mind. But a more accurate description of me would be "*clinging* to the promises."

Honesty compels me to confess, however, that I did not always find the sharing of Scripture a comfort.

On occasion, a well-meaning friend would share the classic verse in Romans 8:28: "God causes all things to work together for good to those who love God." I know the verse, I understand the verse, and I believe the verse. But if I am honest with myself, the first thought I had upon hearing someone quote this verse was, *I wonder if they would feel the same if they stood in my shoes?* I reminded myself that this person had the best of intentions and was only trying to express support. But I found that true compassion goes beyond quoting Scripture, and quoting Scripture is not a substitute for compassion.

Having said that, I will quickly add that when our friend Edie, who has lost two children, quoted Romans 8:28 in her cards and letters, I sat up and listened. She, and others like her, spoke with an authority and life experience that gave meaning to Romans 8:28. It became more than a biblical quote; it was a living offer of hope.

I guess what I am trying to say is that Scripture does indeed remind me of the promises of God, and of course, I know that God is sovereign. But what I needed then and what I need now is not so much to be reminded of His sovereignty but to be reminded of His compassion.

I felt such compassion through the cards, the quiet words of encouragement, the prolonged hugs, the meals dropped off, the polishing of my shoes, the cleaning of my house. Such simple acts of generosity and compassion have touched me deeply and have reminded me of God's unending love.

Lord, thank you for those people who allowed Your Spirit to flow through their hands and feet and ministered to my family and me during the time of our greatest need. Oh that I will forever be a channel of Your compassion to others.

June 16, 2011: Ordering the Grave Markers

While I am writing this journal for my own benefit, I realize that sooner or later my children will read this. Since I finalized plans today for the grave markers, I wanted to document what I did and why.

Before my parents died, I never thought much about the logistical, administrative, and financial implications of a burial. Fortunately, my parents gave a very loving gift many years ago. They made it clear where they wanted to be buried. They also met with a lawyer and completed their wills, living wills, and financial and medical powers of attorney forms. My brothers and I knew exactly what extraordinary measures to take, who would make those decisions, and where our parents wanted to be buried. Not until their deaths did I fully appreciate how loving a gift such actions were. We could focus on grieving and not have to make such difficult decisions, always wondering what they would have wanted. My dad would say you are a fool if you don't make those plans. Actually, he would have said you're a "damn fool."

Tootie and I did not make that mistake.

We too prepared all of the appropriate legal forms and agreed on burial plans. Of course, we assumed it would be years before we would execute any of those plans. We agreed to be buried in the McElhannon family plot with my parents and grandparents (three generations) at Rose Hill Cemetery in Winder, Georgia. We joked that the kids would not visit often, but when they did, they could visit their parents, grandparents, and great-grandparents all at one time.

So, today I finally ordered the grave markers. I had procrastinated about ordering my mom's marker, and in light of Tootie's death, it was just as well. I decided that all the markers should match those of my grandparents. I ordered a replacement for my dad's marker and new ones for my mom and Tootie. At the request of my cousins, I also ordered one each for Uncle Walter and Aunt Ann. Delivery should take about six weeks, but I am glad to get that done. For my children's sake, I even ordered my own marker. Then, all they will have to do is have the date engraved. (Y'all can thank me when you get to heaven.)

As a Christian, I believe that all life is sacred—sacred because we are made in the image of God. Honoring those who have gone before us, in my view, is a way to recognize how sacred life is. It is the right thing to do.

Lord, our bodies are the temple of the Holy Spirit, and I know that once the soul separates from the body, what remains is but a shell. But it also serves as a visible reminder that a life You created existed. Thank you for life: the lives of my parents, my wife, and my children. May I never visit this cemetery without giving thanks and praise to You for the life You gave. After all, You died for us, so that we might live. Thank you, Lord.

June 17, 2011: Friday before Father's Day

I took the afternoon off. I've already planned to take next week off, as most of the kids and I are going to Maine for a family vacation. But today was a rare Friday afternoon, void of meetings or conference calls. I'm outta here, headed to Winder. It's been a month since I last visited the cemetery.

I just needed to go visit awhile.

I didn't really stay long—just long enough to have a cleansing cry. It was one of those times when I let the tears flow while I talked to God. I talked to Tootie too. I wouldn't be a father without her. Oh, how I miss her. This transition from "we" to "I" just doesn't make any sense. There is nothing normal about my "new normal."

I have found these "cleansing cries"—at least that's what I call them—to be a good thing. My heart feels refreshed. No, that's not the right word. It's more like a release of tension or pressure—a release, a relief. Does that make sense?

Oh, Lord, thank you for blessing me with a wife like Tootie and five beautiful children. Having children is a blessing. Having them with her was a joy beyond description. Draw me close, Lord. I need You close.

June 25, 2011: Family Reunion

I flew back from Maine a day early so that I could attend the McElhannon cousins' reunion on Saturday afternoon. I have twenty-three first cousins on my daddy's side. Since almost all of my uncles and aunts have passed on, it's a challenge to get together. My cousin Tamara told me that seeing all of her cousins at Tootie's funeral prompted her and a few others to plan a reunion.

So there we were. It was a great turnout. Most everyone was there. My uncle Bill from Texas, now ninety-two, arrived with two of his children, Joan and Anne. They are staying with me for the next two days.

It was good to be with family.

I saw Carole, who married my cousin Bill. Bill died last summer, so Carole and I have a lot in common at the moment. What is it about shared grief that two people just know what the other is feeling?

June 26, 2011: Remembering Maine

It is hard to believe that the vacation in Maine is already over. Spending time with my family proved to be a joyful respite. It was a bit surreal, doing it without Tootie, as it was my first vacation without her. At times I felt like a fifth wheel. Yet most of the time I felt loved, as I was surrounded by those I love the most. Only Russ and Erin couldn't make it, as they had job commitments.

I will not long forget

- lobster in Maine;
- walks on Scarborough Beach;
- the house at 5 Claudia Way;
- lobster rolls;
- L.L.Bean—all five stores;

40

- walking through Portland;
- blueberry sausage;
- Bob's Clam Shack and Becky's Diner;
- "chowdah";
- seventy degrees and no humidity—in June; and
- being with those I love the most.

These are great memories.

Thank you, Lord, for the gift of family and the joy it brings to be around the fruit of my love with Tootie. You are a gracious God and worthy to be praised.

July 1, 2011: The Book

Well, I finally finished putting together *Walking through the Valley of the Shadow*, the story of Tootie's four-month battle with cancer. It has been a labor of love. I have to admit, writing and compiling this book was a very therapeutic experience. It helped me to focus on something productive, a lasting keepsake. At first I did not intend to share it with anyone outside the immediate family, as my target audience is my future grandchildren. Yet I have had so many requests for copies of the website blog that I finally decided to give out the entire book.

I'm not sure how it will be received.

It has a rather unusual flow, starting with the blog of the last four months of her life, followed by her testimony of faith, and ending with over fifty personal anecdotes and memory stories. I asked the kids to proof it but got very little feedback. It may have been therapeutic for me to write it, but it is still too fresh for them to read it. I understand. Oh, how I understand.

Lord, I ask You to bless those who have supported us throughout the past year. And may those who read Walking through the Valley of the Shadow *be drawn closer to You. Amen.*

July 7, 2011: Feedback

I have started to receive some feedback on the book. It has been rather humbling to realize that even now people are touched by the story.

One particular response caused me to take a deep breath. A lady shared that she woke up at 2:00 a.m. one morning, couldn't go back to sleep, and decided to start reading the book. She didn't stop until she had read it all.

Lord, I give praise to You and am grateful that even months after her death, the story of Tootie's life and death are touching hearts and changing lives. To God be the glory.

July 13, 2011: Church Directory

Tonight I went to church to have my picture taken. Every few years our church publishes a pictorial directory. The first time we'd done this was in the early 1990s, and we took a full family portrait with Tootie and me and our five children. The last time we'd done it was in 2002, and it was just Tootie and I.

This time, it was only me.

Of course, I could have skipped it, as one of my daughters suggested. The problem with a "family" portrait of one is that it reminds you that it is a family portrait of one. The photographer didn't ask if anyone was missing. He didn't have to; my heart had already answered the question. I did not bother waiting to see the proofs. I told them to pick the best one for the directory and left.

July 16, 2011: Sometimes Just Laugh

I ran some errands today. I decided to first get a chicken biscuit at a nearby Bojangles Restaurant. Walking in, I noticed a few folks who looked at me a little longer than usual. I noticed a few more glances as I sat and ate my biscuit.

The next stop was Home Depot. After parking my car, I quickly glanced in my mirror and discovered the source of all those lingering glances. I had cut myself shaving this morning and had put a piece of Kleenex over the spot to help with the clotting. Forgetting to remove it, I had walked into the restaurant with a small piece of tissue stuck on my chin.

Tootie, where are you when I need you?

It's a silly question. I need her every day, all the time. How many times did she save me from looking foolish? Too many to count. Oh well, sometimes you just have to laugh at yourself, even alongside the tears.

July 21, 2011: Grave Markers

Today I left home early and drove to Winder to meet the memorial people at the cemetery. The grave markers, all six of them, were ready to be placed. As I mentioned previously, I ordered them for my parents, Tootie, and myself, as well as for my uncle Walter and aunt Ann. Now, all of the markers match those of my grandparents. I met the workers and made sure they placed the right markers in the proper positions.

It is very strange seeing your own grave marker.

I had to laugh. As I stood there, looking at my own grave marker, I recalled that thirty years ago (1981) Tootie and I had been in Athens waiting for our Mari to be born. Now I was looking forward, wondering where I would be in another thirty years. I only had to look down for the answer. That may sound morbid, but I just laughed and thanked God that the only thing in the grave would be my shell. My spirit, my soul will be with Him.

Here are some words from the hymn, "Be Still My Soul":

> Be still, my soul; the hour is hast'ning on When we shall be forever with the Lord, When disappointment, grief, and fear are gone, Sorrow forgot, love's purest joys restored.
> Be still, my soul: when changes and tears are past, All safe and blessed we shall meet at last.

Thank you, Lord, that the grave is not the end.

July 22, 2011: The Lewis Family

When my daughter Taryn told me that some friends were going to visit them from Virginia, I decided to offer them my home. Jason and Cammie Lewis have three small children, ages seven, four, and two. Taryn and Algernon also came to stay with us. So, for the past week I have had a house filled with five adults and three children. Solitude and quiet were nowhere to be found.

It was a rather joyous diversion, as I had hoped.

Cammie had been a faithful prayer warrior during Tootie's illness, so welcoming her and her family into my home seemed the right thing to do. Yes, it felt good to have some life running through the home.

Lord, thank you for new friends, for the blessing of the fellowship of saints.

July 22, 2011: A Day with the Webbs

As if this week could not have been any busier, I accepted an invitation to play a round of golf with good friend Jim Webb and to have dinner with him, June, and some friends at the Druid Hills Country Club. Later, we attended the performance of *Fiddler on the Roof* at the Fox Theater. Wow, what a full day! Golf, a great meal, and time with friends—I am a man blessed.

July 28, 2011: Six Months

It has been six months since Tootie died. Typing these words is still hard to do. Writing them only triggers my heart to shout as if it has been struck with an ice pick. Sometimes there are just tears, and other times the sobs come forth with such force that I want to scream.

Yes, it still hurts!

Nevertheless, life has fallen into a routine of sorts, most of it good—the kind of "good" that helps you get by one day at a time. Yet reflecting on these past six months still gives me pause. On the surface, it may appear that I have let life come as it does, reacting more than anything to each day's events. But I realize now that some of my prayers of recent months have been answered.

I have been busy. My prayer life has deepened to a new level. I have remained active in church. I have determined to have dinner each week with friends or family or both. I have started exercising, walking one and a half miles a day. I finished Tootie's book, and of course I am writing this journal. So, I guess I have lived the past few months more with a purpose. I think that's a good thing.

July 30, 2011: My Loss, Her Gain

There is immense comfort in knowing that Tootie is with the Lord.

Is she asleep in the Lord, waiting for Resurrection Day, or is she among the "cloud of witnesses" that Scripture mentions? I am not sure of the theology on that point, but in either case, she is with the Lord. My heartache is all about my loss and not her gain. It still hurts, but there remains a comfort in knowing that she is no longer in pain but rather is filled with joy.

Maybe I am just a little jealous. I see through a glass darkly what is to come, while she sees it perfectly clearly. The thought is overwhelming and humbling. How can I not praise the Lord for His grace?

August 2, 2011: Greater Rest

I find myself in a strange place: confident of where Tootie is and where I will be, but still uncertain over the immediate future.

What lies ahead?

I find it hard to think too far into the future. I am still in the one-day-at-a-time mode. But I am finding greater rest for my soul with each passing day. This week, I heard one of my favorite hymns, "Come Thou Fount of Every Blessing." Listening to the words and the familiar tune, I realize how much the third stanza reflects the condition of my heart.

> O to grace how great a debtor daily I'm
> constrained to be!
> Let thy goodness, like a fetter, bind my wandering
> heart to thee.
> Prone to wander, Lord, I feel it, prone to leave the
> God I love; Here's my heart, O take and seal it,
> seal it for thy courts above.

Yes, I may cry out in pain over my loss, even as my heart rejoices in Tootie's gain. *Oh, Lord, bind my wandering heart to Thee; take it, seal it for Thy courts above. Amen.*

> Make me know Thy ways, O LORD; teach me Thy
> paths. Lead me in Thy truth and teach me, for Thou art
> the God of my salvation; for Thee I wait all the day.
> —Psalm 25:4–5

August 4, 2011: Questions without Answers

Over the years, whenever Tootie encountered a tragic or painful event, it usually prompted the age-old question: "Why, Lord?"

She would say to no one in particular, "That's going on my list." She was referring to a mental list of questions she had for the Lord when she got to heaven. One of her questions was "Why did my niece Cindie die at fifteen?" Number one on my list is "Why did Tootie have to die at fifty-nine?" Well, her questions are now answered. Mine are not.

When things happen that I do not understand, I want to shout, accuse, and beg God for answers. If I only knew why, if I only knew that this pain, this suffering, served some higher purpose, maybe I could bear it.

The Scriptures have lots of "why" questions. I guess that's why I so frequently meditate on the Psalms. They seem to be the place where King David and others had such honest dialogues with God.

Yes, Lord, You are my God, for there is no other. I trust You and know that in time I will know the answers to all my questions. But for now, the only Answer I need is You.

Why are you in despair, O my soul? And why have you become disturbed within me? Hope in God, for I shall again praise Him for the help of His presence.
—Psalm 42:5

August 11, 2011: A Delightful Discovery

One of the surprising things I have experienced in the past six months is going through a drawer or a book and discovering a note written by Tootie. More often than not, it was a note she had written to remind herself of something—or as in the case below, a note she had cherished and used as a prayer. Such delightful discoveries they are!

Today I found a Post-it note in her dresser. At the top of it, Tootie had written, "3/27/2009 email from Joy Downing," and the words that followed I can only assume were sent by Joy: "Do not give in to sadness or desperation for what you are going through today. God knows how you feel ... God knows exactly and with perfection what is being allowed to happen to you in your life at this precise moment. God's purpose for you is simply perfect. He wants to show you things that only you can understand by living what you are living and being in the place you are now."

So, I wrote Joy a note, thanking her for her thoughtfulness. Such notes were a tremendous source of encouragement to Tootie. Obviously, these words came at a time when she was dealing with her chronic back pain, eighteen months before we discovered her cancer. I know this meant a lot to her, because she had marked out each *you* in the quote and had replaced it with *I*, making it a personal prayer.

Here is her revised prayer: "Do not give in to sadness or desperation for what *I am* going through today. God knows how *I* feel ... God knows exactly and with perfection what is being allowed to happen to *me* in *my* life at this precise moment. God's purpose for *me* is simply perfect. He wants to show *me* things that only *I* can understand by living what *I am* living and being in the place *I am* now."

How humbled I am to be reminded, oh so frequently, of how these brief notes were simply God's little graces extended to my beloved through generous and compassionate hearts of friends and family. And now, while in the midst of my own year of grief, I have these same words to be a source of encouragement to me. What a God we serve!

Oh, Lord, when it seems that every nook and cranny of this house is a reminder of what I have lost, You bless me with these reminders of Your love for me because of the love Tootie had for You. Thank you for such tender mercies.

> Our hope for you is firmly grounded, knowing
> that as you are sharers of our sufferings, so
> also you are sharers of our comfort.
> —2 Corinthians 1:7

August 16, 2011: Anniversary of Elvis

A news anchor on the radio reminded everyone that today was the thirty-fourth anniversary of the death of Elvis Presley. I could not help but recall where I was when I heard the news: working at my desk in the Chamblee Engineering Office of Southern Bell in 1977.

What is it about great events, that we can visualize exactly what we were doing when they occurred? I vividly recall where I was and what I was doing on the occasions of John F. Kennedy's assassination, Neil Armstrong's walk on the moon, the space shuttle "Challenger" disaster, and of course the Trade Center bombings.

The last two weeks of Tootie's life were a blur, but her last forty-eight hours I can remember by the minute. The whole family gathered around her bed the night of January 27, fully expecting that she would not make it through the evening. I went home about 2:00 a.m., as the girls maintained a vigil. Back at the hospital in the morning, the hospital staff, while cooperative, indicated that we needed to move her to a hospice. While I knew she could not last much longer, plans had to be made. My son Joel graciously helped to make arrangements. We were in a meeting when Maggie called us to "come quickly." By the time I arrived, Tootie was gone.

I must confess a degree of guilt over not being there.

Exhausted, I had been trying to juggle plans for a hospice and a funeral, but in hindsight, I felt I should have been by her side. It is an eternal regret. I have since resigned not to beat myself up over it. The rest of the family was with her, so she was not alone. God knows, and Tootie does too, that I had spent what seemed like every possible hour with her for the previous four months.

What I remember most is that all of our children and their spouses were there, that we comforted one another, and that I was—and am—immensely grateful that our love produced these five great children. Family and faith are never needed more than during times of crisis. Thanks be to God, I had both. Such memories will never be forgotten.

August 19, 2011: The Golf Tournament

I continue to try to balance the quiet times with outside activities. On one hand, I need moments alone to pray, to reminisce, to cry, to heal. But staying active and doing productive things is helpful too. I'm not so busy that I ignore my feelings, but I'm busy enough not to fall into extended periods of melancholy or depression. Staying active at church, doing my daily walks, and being willing to share and speak on occasion help me to cope.

I have decided to once again participate in the annual Refuge Golf Tournament on September 26. This time I am going all-out, hoping to raise at least five thousand dollars in pledges. I sent out an email request today to about 150 folks. I am never really comfortable making such requests, but this year I think everyone understands, and I am optimistic that I will far exceed my goal. I have received so much support during these past six months that the opportunity to be a giver instead of a receiver is a welcome change.

I find that the act of generosity is in itself part of the healing process.

Don't ask me to explain it. I just know that being a giver is a balm to my hurting soul. And helping the ministry that Tootie loved and dedicated her professional career to these past fifteen years is something I want to do. It is something I *have* to do.

August 22, 2011: Group Reunion

This past weekend I attended a conference at church, one of those informal sessions where a guest speaker comes in and spreads three talks and meditation over six hours—a kind of in-house retreat. A year ago, I would not have had time for this, but now—well, now it was a good thing to sit, listen, pray, and share with fellow believers for a few hours.

Bill Warner, a fellow parishioner, invited me to join his men's accountability group (or "Group Reunion," as the Catholic Cursillo Movement calls it). They meet every Monday night at 6:30 p.m., and he said the next one was at his home. I didn't commit to anything, but in my heart I realized that the Lord was again answering one of my prayers. Yes, I was going to go!

Eight of us gathered at the Warners' tonight and spent almost two hours sharing, reading, and praying. The fellowship was warm, encouraging, and a gentle reminder of how much I missed being in a men's prayer group.

Lord, thank you that as we gather together in Your name, You are there among us. Thank you for brothers who are seeking to walk in a way that pleases you. Help me, O Lord, to do the same.

August 25, 2011: Going Home

For thirty-eight-plus years of married life, I always looked forward to returning home after a day of work. No matter what kind of day it had been, driving home and knowing Tootie was there was something I looked forward to each evening. After dealing with five kids all day, I think she looked forward to my coming home too! I always left the work day behind me when I walked into the house. A hug, a kiss, and a conversation about the day's events were soon followed by dinner. Even after the kids were off on their own, coming home never lost its attraction.

Home was the place I felt loved. I felt safe. Maybe that's why, no matter where we were, as long as we were together, we both felt "at home."

Coming home this year has been a roller coaster ride of emotions. Entering an empty house, eating alone, and sleeping alone in a house filled with her pictures is a constant reminder of what used to be. This was a home filled with her presence. Now, it is a house that only echoes her absence. I soon found that focusing on the pain only made things worse with each return trip. Depression awaited with open arms.

My earlier decision to develop a thankful spirit and a heart of gratitude has begun to pay dividends. This house, this home is still a place filled with joyous memories. The more I cherish Tootie's memory, the more thankful I am for the blessing of my wife, and the more this home has become a sanctuary instead of a torture chamber.

Make no mistake: the tears still flow daily, and my heart aches with a pain difficult to explain. Nevertheless, the joy of the Lord is my strength, and memories are something death can never take away.

Thank you, Lord, for the grace that memories give—moments to ponder my blessings of the past. How can I not rejoice in all that You have done? Tootie is now home with You. And in a blink of an eye, I will be going home too. Your open arms await, and once again I will feel safe and loved. Amen!

August 28, 2011: Temptation?

As part of staying active in my church community, I decided last month to start attending my church's adult education class on Sunday morning. This class, titled Catholics 101, is simply a group of parishioners wanting to better understand their faith walk with the Lord. For the last fifteen minutes of today's class, we broke up into groups of five and discussed what each of us considers the greatest temptation hindering our personal relationship with Christ.

Wow, what a question. And they expected us to verbalize it!

After a few moments of contemplating my answer, I realized that I am indeed dealing with a few "temptations." But the lure of the moment is one that few people would really see as a temptation. For me, it's more of a trap.

54

During the course of this year, the dizziness, the numbness, and the heartache have been, at times, overwhelming. I just want to escape and be alone. The temptation is to turn on the TV and watch a few hours of *NCIS* reruns. That is so easy to do. Now, to be frank, I have not watched hours of reruns, although I have spent an occasional evening as a couch potato. My commitment to a regular devotional life has been a holy detour keeping me on track. Every evening, I stop and read my two daily devotionals, look up the associated Scripture, and pray, and pray, and pray.

O Lord, I thirst for You. Yes, the heartache and grief may indeed be a reminder that this world does not fully satisfy. You and You alone meet all my needs. Let me be a prayer warrior for others as they have been for my family and me.

August 30, 2011: Whispers That Echo

I woke up in the middle of the night last evening. I thought I heard Tootie's voice. Oh, how I miss her, how I miss hearing her voice. She was such an encourager to me, so compassionate, so tender. I could always tell by the tone of her voice how she was doing.

A whisper is such an intimate act.

How many times did Tootie rest her arm on my shoulder, lean her head close, and whisper into my ear. Those whispers more often than not were simply a tender comment or an "I love you." Those shared intimate moments are a treasure beyond words. The softest of spoken words now echo in my mind years later, never to be forgotten, savored for a lifetime.

September 2, 2011: Number 39

Well, today finally came. Since 1972, I have been able to recall where I spent every September 2—always with Tootie—until today. Today is our wedding anniversary. I must admit, it has been an emotional day. Yes, today is a special day and one I have looked forward to with mixed emotions. I didn't know that #38 would be the last one together or that #39 would be the first one without her.

I purposed to take today off from work. Yes, it is the Friday before the Labor Day weekend, and any other year I probably would be taking it off so we could go somewhere or spend a long weekend with family at Lake Oconee. But not this year.

Today, I had a date with my beloved—at Rose Hill Cemetery in Winder.

Son Joel invited me to come by his home in Athens this evening. He needed help moving some furniture and offered dinner as an enticement. Son Russ was coming to help, as well. While I was tempted to spend all day alone with my memories, I reconsidered. What better way to spend the evening meal than with two of our children, the fruit of our marriage?

But first, the cemetery called.

I left home around noon and headed to Winder. On the way, I picked up yellow roses—her favorite—and then spent some time standing over the sacred ground at Rose Hill.

Memories of our wedding day started to flow. Tootie always enjoyed giving me grief about September 2 being our wedding day. She said it was because Georgia Tech didn't have a football game that weekend. Our rehearsal dinner was also moved from a Friday to a Thursday night, because our high school alma mater's first game of the season was on Friday. All of this is true, but I do not recall her objecting to it at the time. She just enjoyed telling people our wedding was scheduled around football. Nevertheless, it has always made the Labor Day weekend a fun time.

I recalled our first anniversary. We were living in the basement apartment of Tootie's parents' home. Since I still had a year to go before graduating from Georgia Tech, and Tootie was due to deliver Joel in July, we had moved in with her parents in the spring of 1973. When we celebrated anniversary number one, Joel was almost two months old. We defrosted the wedding cake saved from the wedding and enjoyed it one last time.

Recalling those anniversaries during our thirty-eight years, four months, and twenty-six days of marriage had the unexpected effect of putting a smile on my tearstained face. How blessed a man I was. How blessed a man I am! Even if I had known that her life would be cut short, I would not have traded those years for anyone else.

I guess most folks will think I am being overly sentimental, but I stopped and bought her one last anniversary card. As I laid the roses down, I slipped the card underneath the concrete vase. I added a note: "#39 is not the same without you. But, oh my, #1 to #38 were fantastic. Love ya bunches, B"

Lord, I give thanks to You for the blessing of marriage and for the way You blessed me through the love of this woman. Recalling how we delighted in loving each other only reminds me that such a love is meant to reflect the delight You have in Your bride, the church. Oh, that I find my joy in You.

Delight yourself in the LORD and He will
give you the desires of your heart.
—Psalm 37:4

September 3, 2011: Saturday: A Busy Day

Today turned out to be a busy day. This is probably a good thing, as again I was tempted to sit quietly in a chair all day and ponder the past. I did my usual Saturday morning walk with John Kommeth and then returned home in time to meet with Ronnie, the furniture refinisher, who came by to pick up our church pew that we had saved from our time at Saint Joseph Church in Athens. I am having it refinished and cut down to a reasonable size.

Later, I picked up the rocker I am giving to Maggie as a baby gift. This rocker is the sole remaining piece of living room furniture from a set my mom and dad gave us as a wedding gift in 1972. Now that the cushions are redone, it only seemed fitting to pick it up on the anniversary weekend of our marriage. I later spoke with Maggie and Taryn and planned on having dinner with them on Sunday and Monday, respectively. I also decided to attend Mass at 5:00 p.m. Getting there about twenty minutes early allowed time for meditation and prayer.

My soul needed the nourishment.

One thing most people do not know is that after our wedding in 1972, Tootie and I did not go directly to the Stone Mountain Inn. We drove in the opposite direction—to the Monastery of the Holy Spirit in Conyers. Father Richard Kieran, who officiated our wedding, had returned to a Cursillo retreat that was in progress at the monastery. We arrived and walked to the chapel below the main sanctuary and spent some time in prayer before finally heading to Stone Mountain. Prayer was a foundation for all that would come. Tootie and I really wanted our marriage to get off to the right start. Little did we know that we would later spend the last twenty-three years of Tootie's life in Conyers, just a few miles from the monastery.

I cherish those memories. Yes, they bring tears to my eyes, but much like the meditation in church, they nourish my soul. I am slowly learning how to handle the memories, how to cherish them rather than spending all day in a dark corner grieving over what I have lost. Instead, I cling to my lifeline, my hope, the Lord Jesus.

September 4, 2011: Death, Where Is Your Sting?

I love providential coincidences. Is that an oxymoron? If it's providential, is it a coincidence? All I know is that there have been times too numerous to mention when the light of a devotional, an article, or a conversation has pierced the foggy darkness at the precise moment my soul hungered for a taste of grace.

Today was such a day.

I receive a daily "Viewpoint" email from the Colson Center for Christian Worldview. Today the commentary came from T. M. Moore, titled "Death Shall Be No More—Where Is Your Sting?" So, here I am struggling through this weekend—the first anniversary in thirty-eight years that Tootie and I are apart—and the sting of death, her death, feels like a sizzling-hot branding iron upon my heart, when I happen to read this commentary. Coincidence?

I had met the author, T. M. Moore, during my Centurion training in 2007. Tall, slim, and looking more like a professor than a preacher, his delivery comes across like a wise uncle imparting wisdom gleaned from a life lived in service to the Lord. I could actually remember the sound of his voice as I read through his commentary.

Quoting Revelation 21:3–4, he reminded the reader that there will come a time when "death will be no more." It was a reminder that while we are now prone to be "self-centered, short-sighted, foolish, and materialistic, and perpetually prone to disappoint ourselves and others," there will come a time when death will not affect us, when we are "inclined to give, serve, encourage, affirm, support, and enjoy one another. Forever!"

That is our hope as believers: that when death loses its sting, "we shall live forever through and with our Lord Jesus Christ."

Death will be no more. Oh, how I long for that day. No more tears, no more pain. No more sting.

Thank you, Lord, for these little graces that so often have come through the loving hands of a friend, an encouraging word from a coworker, or even an email from an electronic version of a devotional. Reminders of a time when death will be no more also remind me of the reason I accepted Your invitation to follow You. Amen.

The people who walk in darkness will
see a great light; those who live in a dark
land, the light will shine on them.
—Isaiah 9:2

September 10, 2011: Robert Duvall, Golf, and Utopia

I went to a movie last night. It was such an experience that I had to come home and write my reflection upon it. Over the years, I have found simple pleasure in writing what I call a "reflection" of an event or an experience. I hope that one day my children will find these brief anecdotes interesting and inspiring—or at least amusing.

As I wrote it, I realized that I needed to share it with other people. I'm not sure I can explain it; I just felt compelled to do so. So I drafted the following and emailed it out to about a hundred folks. I'll include it here too, as it reflects yet another aspect of my grieving process.

Robert Duvall, Golf, and Utopia

On a whim, I went to a movie last night. I went expecting to be entertained, but I came away with much more. It was an unusual experience, one I am compelled to write down and share. Part reflection, part movie review, it is a 100 percent heartfelt response to what I saw.

I had seen a movie trailer about the new Robert Duvall film called *Seven Days in Utopia*. Robert Duvall and golf—whoa, Nellie! That's an actor and plot combination I could not resist, much less wait until it showed up as a video rental. Now, you must understand that Tootie and I did not go to movies very often. Of course, only a year ago, she would have been sitting there with me, enjoying this picture and whispering in my ear with mock seriousness about my golf game: "Do you play like that?"

I am not sure I can remember the last time I went to a theater alone, but I am sure it was during puberty! But alone I went, thinking that enjoying a good movie in a crowd of Duvall and golf fans just might be a delightful way to spend two hours. However, to my amazement, the local theater was not overrun with teens on a Friday date night. An even greater surprise awaited. I entered the screening room for *Utopia*, only to discover that it was empty. As I watched through an endless series of previews, I expected more Duvall fans to join me, but as the opening credits began, I realized that I was completely alone in the theater ... on a Friday night. Unbelievable.

How do you get lost in a crowd of one? Being an audience of one only reminds you that you are an audience of one, and oh how I was already missing those sweet whispers I could always depend on hearing during a show. Was the Devil mocking me? I could almost hear his laughter at my solitary state. But what is meant for evil can be turned to good.

Unintended though it may have been, I realized that I was about to enjoy a private showing of this movie. Was it coincidence that I was alone in the theater? Was it an opportunity for the Devil to mock my aloneness? Or maybe, just maybe, it was one of those little moments of grace when your soul is about to be nourished without distractions.

The very first screen shot caught my attention. It was a Scripture verse, Isaiah 30:21: "And your ears shall hear a word behind you, 'This is the way, walk in it,' whenever you turn to the right or to the left." Hmmm ... the movie *Secretariat* had opened with a Scripture verse, so maybe this movie had more depth than just Robert Duvall and golf.

To be honest, this movie will not win any Academy Awards. Nevertheless, I quickly became engrossed in this story about life and redemption and spending *Seven Days in Utopia*. You see, the main character, Luke, is a young pro golfer who has just experienced a meltdown on the last hole of a tournament. Angry and embarrassed, he hurriedly leaves the course and drives away in no particular direction, until he comes to a fork in the road and takes the road that goes through Utopia. I won't give away the entire plot, but Luke ends up spending a week in this small community, and during those seven days, he is tutored by Johnny (played by Duvall), a former player himself. Johnny starts out teaching Luke about golf, but in the process Luke learns how to handle adversity and disappointment. He learns about life, faith, and truth.

I was particularly impressed by how the movie ended. I'll simply use the same phrase I read in the move review at Pluggedin.com. The movie "makes its final and perhaps best point through quiet understatement."

Yes, I went to the movie because of Robert Duvall and golf. But I left encouraged to listen to the "voice of truth" and reminded that the most important things in life are not things.

You might want to consider a road trip to Utopia too. I am glad I did. Maybe I was not so alone after all.

Thank you, Lord, for Your compassion. I was so hesitant to go out by myself last night. I am still amazed at how it turned out. You speak to my heart in so many ways. I really do not understand it all, but thankfully I don't have to. Your ways are higher than mine. In You and You alone I trust. Amen.

For as the heavens are higher than the earth,
so are My ways higher than your ways and
My thoughts than your thoughts.
—Isaiah 55:9

September 10, 2011: The Old Neighborhood

I rarely put two entries into this journal on the same day, but today is an unusual day. John Kommeth and I met for our usual Saturday morning walk, but due to his schedule, I agreed to meet him at his house and just walk through his neighborhood. However, his neighborhood, Meadowbrook Subdivision, is the same neighborhood where Tootie and I lived from 1988 to 2003.

Walking through the familiar streets flooded my mind with memories. We walked by the local Barksdale Elementary School, where Maggie and Mari attended when we first moved to Conyers. We passed dozens of homes where friends lived or used to live, where we'd had block parties and had taken walks ourselves. Then we walked by our old home. The current owner had let everything grow up so much that you could barely tell he had repainted it an awful blue color.

I could have stood at the curb and stared at the yard I had cut, the windows I had installed, and the trees I had planted. I could have recalled with ease all the memories that fifteen years held.

But no, I did not stop and stare. I merely slowed down, looked to my right, smiled, and kept walking.

This was the past—a joyful past for sure, and one that overflows with the fondest of memories.

I refuse to let such instances break my heart. I am just thankful that here is a place where Tootie and I loved our family and loved each other, a place that will always hold cherished memories of the past.

Lord, I know this home on Ridgedale Lane is only wood and glass, but it was a house we made a home. One day, it will pass away, but the lives that were changed in that home will never pass away. Those are the memories I delight in, because I know they are what delight You too. Amen.

September 16, 2011: A Day of Encouragement

Some days my tears flow like a flood. Psalm 42:3 says it all: "My tears have been my food day and night, while they say to me all day long, 'Where is your God?'" Then there are days like today, when encouragement comes from so many different sources.

Today I read a quote from the book *Notes from the Tilt-A-Whirl* by N. D. Wilson:

> God has the authority to shape a soul with his voice, bind it to matter, and send it into history. And he has the authority to sever my soul from my body and call it to another part of the stage. He has the authority to reuse the matter from my flesh in daffodils. I'm not worried. I'll get more.

There is no evil in his voice calling us to cross the Jordan, whether he calls us singly or in droves. There is no evil when he tells us to lay our first flesh down, no more than when he sends a caterpillar into its cocoon.

To his eyes, you never leave the stage. You do not cease to exist. It is a chapter ending, an act, not the play itself. Look to him. Walk toward him. The cocoon is a death, but not a final death. The coffin can be a tragedy, but not for long.

There will be butterflies.

I will die, and when I do—whether it be in my bed as age creeps over me, or struck by lightning, a meteor, or a UPS truck—[God's] hand will be the one that cuts the thread and shows me the path he blazed through tragedy. His finger will point to the parade.

Reading this brought me a great sense of comfort, not only about Tootie but about myself. Trusting God somehow removes the fear of death.

Later in the evening, as I prepared for bed, I sat down, as is my usual custom, for a time of reading and prayer. The Scripture in my evening devotional was Psalm 139:3–18:

For Thou didst form my inward parts; Thou didst weave me in my mother's womb. I will give thanks to Thee, for I am fearfully and wonderfully made; wonderful are Thy works, and my soul knows it very well. My frame was not hidden from Thee, when I was made in secret, and skillfully wrought in the depths of the earth; Thine eyes have seen my unformed substance; and in Thy book were all written the days that were ordained for me, when as yet there was not one of them. How precious also are Thy thoughts to me, O God! How vast is the sum of them! If I should count them, they would outnumber the sand. When I awake, I am still with Thee.

My thoughts first jumped to daughter Maggie, as her baby is now almost twenty weeks in utero. That baby is being fearfully and wonderfully made. But verse 16 caught my attention, especially in light of this morning's reading: "Thine eyes have seen my unformed substance; and in Thy book were all written the days that were ordained for me, when as yet there was not one of them."

God knew the number of days that were ordained for Tootie, just as He does for me. Wow! Then verses 17 and 18 reminded me of how precious are God's thoughts of me.

Somehow, this morning's reading and the one tonight combined to overwhelm me with a sense of God's plan, God's love, and God's presence.

Thank you, Lord, for Your lovingkindness. I am overwhelmed. Your thoughts of me outnumber the grains of sand. Forgive me for those times You seem so far away. Reading Psalm 139 only emphasizes how personal, how intimate a God You are. Thank you for loving me unconditionally. Amen.

September 17, 2011: Day of Joy

Being with family to celebrate life events has been a great consolation this year. This past Thursday, our son Joel was recognized at a luncheon as an honoree of the University of

Georgia Alumni Associations' first inaugural class of the "Top 40 Graduates under 40." Today, in a pregame ceremony, he, along with the other honorees, were recognized on the field of Sanford Stadium prior to the UGA-Coastal Carolina football game. This is far more than just a distraction from grief. It is a true celebration of joy at the accomplishments of a child, one the whole family enjoyed on Thursday and Saturday. I just love it when our children turn out for each other.

One reason I rejoice so much is that I know Tootie loved this kind of thing. By that I mean that she would be absolutely delighted to see one of her children recognized in this way, to see her family support each other in times of crisis or, like Thursday and today, in a time of celebration.

I cannot help but recall those early days of raising our family. We had made the conscious decision to have our children early, and Tootie gladly put her nursing career on hold to be a full-time mom.

During almost ten years of diapers, night feedings, and crying babies, the two of us did pause occasionally to reflect upon our earlier decision and ponder our current priorities. Not that she or I would have changed anything. Oh, those early years of parenting produced many precious moments, but we both knew that the sacrifices we were making would not bear fruit for years to come.

There have been many times these past few years when seeing the kind of adults our children had become not only validated her sacrifice but brought joy to her heart. Today would have been such a day for her. It certainly was for me.

September 21, 2011: Rest

One of my favorite John Wayne movies is a little-known 1947 film, titled *Angel and the Badman*. John Wayne plays a supposedly bad guy named Quirt Evans who is shot by the real bad guys early in the opening scenes. He is then nursed back to health by a Quaker family. Of course, he later falls in love with the beautiful daughter.

In one of the early movie scenes, Quirt is brought, wounded, into the Quaker family home. Lying in bed, he is unconscious, but he is obviously unable to rest, as his body moves and rolls about as if he is having a nightmare. The father of the Quaker family quickly recognizes the problem. He pulls Quirt's gun from his holster by the bed, removes the bullets, and places the gun in the unconscious gunfighter's hand. Quirt instantly relaxes and falls into a deep sleep.

It took a familiar touch to calm his restless spirit.

I know the feeling. If I am honest, I will admit that a good night's sleep has been a rather unusual occurrence this year. Either I have trouble going to sleep, or I wake up at 2:30 a.m., or I wake up at 5:00 a.m., or all of the above. I don't need a gun to hold. I just need Tootie.

We had a habit of falling asleep touching one another. Sometimes we held hands or had one hand lying on the other. If she lay on her side, I would rest my hand on her hip. More often than not, I would slide my foot over until it rested right up against the underside of her foot. Or better yet, we would cuddle. We were champion cuddlers.

So sleeping alone has been a change to which I have not yet fully adjusted. I cry with the psalmist in 22:2: "Oh my God, I cry by day, but Thou dost not answer; and by night, but I have no rest."

O Lord, You are my hope, my peace, my salvation. In You alone will I trust and rest my weary soul. Be my strength, my Rock. Amen.

Return to your rest, O my soul, for the LORD has dealt
bountifully with you. For Thou hast rescued my soul
from death, my eyes from tears, my feet from stumbling.
—Psalm 116:7–8

September 29, 2011: One Year Ago

It's Thursday, and tomorrow I leave for a weekend at Jekyll Island. My good friend Fred Cassidy and I have been making this annual journey to the Georgia Bell Classic golf tournament for ten years. It's a great chance to see old friends who have retired from "Ma Bell" and enjoy a few rounds of golf. Last year would have been our tenth trip. I say "would have been," because one year ago today was when Tootie and I confirmed her cancer.

I remember it vividly. Following her mammogram, an ultrasound, and a biopsy, we were told to expect results on Thursday, September 30. Having made reservations two months earlier, Fred and I were planning to leave on Friday, October 1, for Jekyll. But I had called Fred earlier in the week and, expecting the worse, told him there was no way I would leave Tootie alone that weekend.

We canceled our trip.

Sure enough, we got the bad news and spent the weekend stunned and coming to grips with what might lie ahead. Oh my, we had no idea what was coming.

Now, a year later, I was taking today (Thursday) and Friday off. It was time for another visit to Rose Hill Cemetery.

Dear friend Dick Willits had expressed interest in going along sometime, so I gave him a call and invited him to join me. It might be good to have some company on this trip.

It was a beautiful fall day. Once there, I pointed out all the family plots, and we quietly stood beside my beloved's grave. Dick began to pray his prayers, and I stood by quietly. Once done, he graciously stepped away and allowed me some private time to once again water this sacred ground with a few tears. I always leave some of myself with Tootie on each visit.

We took the long way home and drove through Athens. I wanted Dick to see Joel and Rosemary's home—and especially their new deck. Dick is a woodworker, so I knew he would delight in seeing the craftsmanship of everything they had done. Rosemary was there to greet us, and Dick was indeed surprised and delighted with all he saw.

Tomorrow, it's off to Jekyll Island, but today was a day to remember, to reflect, and to give thanks. I cannot help but be in awe of the thirty-eight years of marriage I had with Tootie. Yes, I have lost much, but oh what a blessed man I am. Yes, this week has been a tough one, as these one-year-old memories are like a sharp slap in the face. But having friends like Fred and Dick is God's blessing too.

Lord, thank you for the blessings of friends with whom I can share my sorrow. A man is rich if he has one such friend, and you have blessed me with many. I praise You, Lord, for being a God of compassion. Amen.

October 10, 2011: The Divine Grace of the Holy Ache

Here it is, a lovely fall day, and I sit pondering. I find myself doing that on many an occasion, sometimes to simply cherish a memory, and other times, to contemplate the future.

Mostly, it is to come to grips with how to take the next step.

Grief will not long be ignored, and I continue to embrace and accept it, but I endeavor, with the Lord's help, to work through it. Pondering allows time to process the dramatic changes that have taken place this past year.

Today, I pondered the concept of what I call the "Holy Ache."

It occurred to me that if marriage is a sacrament, then marriage is a sacred union, a sacred relationship. When death breaks that holy union, it is a natural thing for grief to follow. It is more than a sense of loss, as if you misplaced a valuable ring or even lost a job. This is a Holy Ache, a pain deep in your soul that cannot be easily consoled.

As I look at others who have suffered the same, I see some who have handled it well and others who have tried to stop the pain through counterfeit measures—like buying more "things," quickly remarrying, or seeking relief through drugs or alcohol.

But this grief runs deep, and relief can be found in only one place.

A sacred relationship was lost. It requires a spiritual solution to be restored. The Lord is my Rock, my Light, my firm foundation. God's comfort, and His alone, helps me see what the Holy Ache really is: a reminder that this is not the way it is supposed to be.

One day will be that day when there are no more tears, no more pain, and no more Holy Ache.

Lord, I have never loved You more. Oh, how the comfort and joy You give now is but a foretaste of what is to come. Thank you for being my redeemer, my comforter, and my friend. Amen.

> Behold, the tabernacle of God is among men, and
> He shall dwell among them, and they shall be His
> people, and God Himself shall be among them,
> and He shall wipe away every tear from their eyes;
> and there shall no longer be any death; there shall
> no longer be any mourning, or crying, or pain.
> —Revelation 21:3–4

October 16, 2011: The Glorious Gift

Soon after the funeral, I committed myself to faithfully having a devotional time every evening. I read from a couple of devotionals, look up the associated Scriptures, and pray using the Scriptures to guide my words. The devotional, *Jesus Calling*, is one that Tootie and I used those last three months of her life. I have continued to read it, even now. It was written in first person from the perspective of Jesus, as if He was talking directly to us. I have lost count of the number of times it has spoken in a powerful way to the need of the moment. Tonight may have been the most profound of any evening.

The sense of loss is, at times, still overwhelming. To say I need encouragement to keep getting up every morning is an understatement. I simply refuse to allow despair to overwhelm me, and the only way I know to do that is to rest in the Lord and seek to serve Him.

Tonight I read the following for the October 16 entry in *Jesus Calling*:

> Look to Me continually for help, comfort, and companionship. Because I am always by your side, the briefest glance can connect you with Me. When you look to Me for help, it flows freely from My Presence. This recognition of your need for Me, in small matters as well as in large ones, keeps you spiritually alive.
>
> When you need comfort, I love to enfold you in My arms. I enable you to not only feel comforted but also to be a channel through whom I comfort others. Thus you are doubly blessed, because a living channel absorbs some of whatever flows through it.
>
> My constant Companionship is the *pièce de résistance*: the summit of salvation blessings. No matter what losses you experience in your life, no one can take away this glorious gift.
>
> I sought the LORD, and He answered me,
> And delivered me from all my fears.
> They looked to Him and were radiant,
> And their faces will never be ashamed.
> This poor man cried, and the LORD
>   heard him
> And saved him out of all his troubles
>   (Psalm 34:4–6).
>
> Seek the LORD and His strength;
> Seek His face continually (Psalm 105:4).

*Oh, Lord, I do seek You and need your comfort and companionship.
What a blessing to have a gift I can never lose. Amen.*

October 24, 2011: "No Turning Back"

The cynic will likely laugh at all of my musings. Each coincidence I attribute to God's grace will no doubt elicit a huge guffaw from the jaded skeptic. But I care not how others may construe my response to the almost daily sources of encouragement.

I am convinced that God speaks to me in so many ways that I have but to open my eyes and heart to discover a new avenue by which He is telling me, "I love you. I am with you. I will never leave you."

In the October 22, 2011, edition of *WORLD* magazine, I found such a love note. Andree Seu's commentary, titled "No Turning Back," recounted the response of Scott and Janet Willis to the tragic loss of their six children in a car fire. These heartbroken parents actually interpreted Psalm 34:1, "I will bless the Lord at all times," to mean that they should bless the Lord at *all* times. They took Scripture at face value, and clinging to the words of the Psalmist, they chose to praise God. Seu writes, "Praise meets trauma where nothing else can reach. Praise in the face of devastation releases blessings obtainable in no other way. The presence of God is directly related to worship."

I confess to being deeply touched by this story. As noted earlier this year, I have chosen, against all that I feel, to express gratitude and thanksgiving to God for the blessings of what I have had rather than to curse Him for what I have lost. For some reason, this article helped me to see this in perspective. Blessing the Lord at *all* times, as hard as that is, is true worship. And in the midst of such praise, God is present in all comfort and healing.

Thank you, Lord, for Your daily graces. Never allow me to be so busy or so focused on my problems that I fail to recognize the simple ways You choose to reach out and gently wash my soul in Your love. Amen.

I will bless the Lord at all times; His praise
shall continually be in my mouth.
—Psalm 34:1

October 29, 2011: Treasures in a Box

Taryn and Mari have decided to give their sister Maggie a baby shower—at my house. This is no surprise. It is a large shower, and few other places can handle the expected crowd. So I decided to have the carpets cleaned. They are way overdue for a good cleaning. I can almost hear Tootie chuckling and saying, "It's about time." Let's just say that such activities were an occasional bone of contention between us. She always had more ideas than I had energy to do them.

Getting the master bedroom closet ready for the cleaning, I came across another box of notes, cards, and letters that Tootie had tucked away. I spent tonight going through them. I have stated that she was not one to keep a journal, but she did occasionally go through a season where she documented her thoughts and prayers. Such was the case during a six-month period in 1999 when she had written down her prayers for family and friends. Reading these decade-old offerings was a heartwarming experience.

The year 1999 was a tough one for me professionally. My job was overwhelming, and I would leave at 6:00 each morning and not return until 7:00 to 8:00 each night. Tootie and I had frequently talked and prayed about this burden. Seeing her passionate prayers for me in written form provoked more than just a reliving of the period; they produced a tearful and joyous response. Blessed is the man who has such a wife.

In the same box were some love notes from when we were in college, and even a few pictures from our high school graduation trip to Daytona Beach in Florida. Tootie's parents, along with another couple, had chaperoned the girls. I and five other guys had hung around their motel and enjoyed a week of fun in the sun. Seeing pictures of that trip brought back a treasure trove of memories. Reliving memories of a decade ago *and* those of four decades ago was an odd experience. Seeing the evidence of young teenage love that blossomed into my finding a godly woman who would pray for her husband some thirty years later—well, those are precious memories that I gratefully cherish.

Thank you, Lord, again and again, for the blessing of a godly wife. Reading her notes and prayers fills my heart with gratitude. You and You alone are sufficient to meet my deepest needs. Amen.

Now to Him who is able to do far more abundantly
beyond all that we ask or think, according to
the power that works within us, to Him be
the glory in the church and in Christ Jesus to
all generations, for ever and ever. Amen.
—Ephesians 3:20–21

October 30, 2011: Good Conversation

It's been nine months. In some ways, it seems like a lifetime. In others, it feels as if it happened yesterday. I have been sailing in uncharted waters this year, and the fog has lifted only slightly.

Planning ahead—even thinking about planning ahead—is still beyond my grasp. The holidays approach, as does the one-year anniversary of Tootie's passing.

These are mountains I must climb before I can see the next horizon.

There is so much I miss about Tootie. In the past decade, when the two of us finally had a chance to travel, we most enjoyed those four- to seven-hour drives to Charleston, Myrtle Beach, Hilton Head, or Nashville. We would listen to a CD, usually a Focus on the Family radio program, and then Tootie would sneak in a nap somewhere along the way. In between, we talked, laughed, reminisced, and planned ahead. I never grew tired of conversation with her. She had a way of making me feel like I was the most important person in the world to her. She possessed a reservoir of common sense, and I realized long ago that to ignore her perspective or advice was never a good idea.

Her sense of vision far exceeded mine. So, when we talked about where we wanted to retire or what we wanted to do after I retired, her insights tended to guide the discussion. It reminded me of the time when, as a teenager, I would practice tennis by hitting the tennis ball against the brick carport wall at my home. It always bounced back, but not always where I expected it.

Conversations with Tootie were a lot like that tennis ball.

They always bounced back, but sometimes with a different perspective or direction than I expected. Early in our marriage, these diverse perspectives were initially annoying, if not frustrating. But as time went by, I grew to appreciate how her insights challenged me to expand my horizons too. Now, without her, it just seems like I hit the ball and it never returns.

Lord, I am not quite sure how to express my thoughts right now. This season of grief has driven me to You. I know I cannot do this alone. Thank you for being a God who cares and who is always there.

November 9, 2011: Last Psalms Class

One of the things I have grown to appreciate during this year of grief is the book of Psalms. How is it that these prayers, written three thousand years ago, so express the feelings within my heart? I was drawn to them in the last months of Tootie's life, and they have been a frequent rest stop for me virtually every day this year. Yes, the Psalms have given a voice to the agony within my soul.

So, when a ten-week study of Psalms was offered at my parish, I could not resist the opportunity. Tonight was the final class. I can truly say that I have not been disappointed. I learned so much, kind of like discovering that a diamond you thought was only one carat is actually one hundred carats. Such richness and depth, the Psalms are so much more than what they first appear. I found more than comfort. I found a voice.

> Let the words of my mouth and the meditation
> of my heart be acceptable in Thy sight, O
> LORD, my rock and my Redeemer.
> —Psalm 19:14

November 11, 2011: I Miss the Kiss

One of the things I loved about being married to Tootie was the anticipation that would build from the moment I left the office until I walked through our door to be greeted by her welcoming smile, a warm embrace, and a gentle kiss. I knew I was now on safe ground in my home, my castle. Now, this was not a castle where I ruled. Anyone who knew Tootie would laugh at the thought. No, I use the term *castle* in the sense of a place where I knew I was loved. My home was a place of safety and security. I could close the door on all the trials and tribulations outside, knowing that inside I could let my guard down.

Our home was a place of love.

As noted in previous posts, in the weeks and months after her funeral, coming home proved to be a different experience: no hug, no kiss. Oh, how I miss that kiss. Coming home to an empty castle was a daily reminder of what I had lost. Instead of a place of refuge, it was a chamber of painful memories.

That has slowly begun to change.

I can't tell exactly when it happened, but I have grown increasingly aware that coming home has lost most of its bite. Yes, the house is still empty. Yes, loneliness and grief still stalk my every move. But as I have sought the Lord in daily prayer, as I have cried out before Him, I have sensed a healing, a comfort of my broken spirit. I look forward to those sacred moments when I sit on the couch, read my devotionals, look up the Scripture passages, and commune with my Lord. It is a routine as regular as that evening kiss.

Maybe that's it. My evening's devotional has become like that daily kiss, where I am reminded that I am loved beyond description. My home may still be my castle, but now it is simply a reminder that the Lord is my refuge, my rock, and my shelter.

Thank you, Lord. Thank you, Holy Spirit, that Your indwelling presence has nurtured my shattered soul. I bless Your name.

November 13, 2011: The Whistle

I whistled today. I don't remember the last time I whistled a tune.

Once I realized I was whistling, I stopped, keenly aware that something was different. Whistling, to me, always reflected a happy mood. So, when I caught myself whistling a tune, I had to ask myself why I was doing it.

I was conscious that I had hummed some hymns in recent months, but more as a lament, a prayer, seeking God's comforting presence. But a whistle? That was a different thing altogether. My only explanation is that I have a greater sense of peace.

November 16, 2011: Dinner with Sister Margaret

A couple of months ago, I received an email from our longtime friend Sister Margaret McAnoy. Tootie and I had met this nun from Michigan in the early seventies when we were involved in Cursillo. She had such a gentle and compassionate spirit that we always felt comfortable in her presence. Our daughter Maggie is actually named after her.

Her email suggested we get together for dinner and reminisce. Tonight, we did exactly that. We met at the Red Lobster restaurant on LaVista Road, and dinner turned into a two-hour conversation. I shared with her pictures of Maggie's wedding. She recalled a few favorite memories, asked me several questions about how I was doing, but mostly just listened patiently as I rambled from one topic to another. In hindsight, I think I did most of the talking, yet I left feeling uplifted and encouraged in my spirit.

Driving home, I reflected on how much this evening represented what so many other brothers and sisters in Christ have done for me these past ten months. Their kindness, love, and support have shielded me from the cold embrace of grief and have provided comfort like a warm blanket on a chilly night. They have been a living expression of the "one another" verses in Scripture.

Jesus told his followers in John 13:34–35 to "love one another." The Word is filled with many such admonitions.

- Serve one another (Galatians 5:13).
- Bear one another's burdens (Galatians 6:2).
- Pray for one another (James 5:16).
- Seek after that which is good for one another (1 Thess. 5:15).

Lord, thank you for loving me through so many of your children. I cannot go on alone. I cannot do this alone. I have not the strength or even the will to get out of bed each day, much less take a step. Nevertheless, You are my strength, my hope. Thank you for your church, the body of Christ, who seek to serve you by loving one another, especially those in need. Help me, O Lord, to do the same.

Therefore encourage one another
and build up one another.
—1 Thessalonians 5:11

November 22, 2011: Heaven Is for Real

In our adult education class this past Sunday, one of our deacons recommended a book, *Heaven Is for Real*. This book is about the out-of-body experience of a young boy. Near death, he survived.

Some months later, his dad discovered in conversation with the four-year-old that he had met Jesus. The book details this lad's experience. I found this remarkable book to be a great comfort.

I realize that my desire to have Tootie back is a selfish one.

She is now out of pain and in the presence of the Lord. Wanting her back is for my benefit, certainly not hers. Christians have a hope, a certain hope of life after death. While I am confident in this Christian doctrine, I will candidly admit that reading this book flooded my soul with a sense of joy and wonder.

I could easily imagine Tootie sitting with Jesus. Reading the story of this young boy brought tears to my eyes and joy to my heart. Tootie is *really* with the Lord. How can I not rejoice? Even through my tears, through my pain, I praise God that He is a God of love, a God who keeps His promises, a God who loves us far more than we can imagine. Yes, I had a foretaste of heaven, and it was sweet.

Thank you, Lord, for this glimpse into eternity. Oh, that I might walk in a way that pleases You and brings joy to Your heart as much as knowing that my Tootie is with You brings joy to mine.

November 24, 2011: Thanksgiving Day

How do I describe today? If I am honest with myself, I must admit that I approached this holiday much like I did our anniversary date. I just wanted to get through it. That may not be the best approach, but part of me wanted to get it over with. Yet it remains a day to give thanks.

Maggie was gracious enough to invite me down, and I was able to spend the day with family. The food was good, and the company was even better. I felt loved and grateful for all of the above.

The most emotional moment occurred on my ride home. Leaving about 7:00 p.m. for the one-hour drive back to Conyers, I kept the radio off and drove in silence. I did not want any distractions. How many times in the past twenty-five years had Tootie and I made this same journey along Interstate 20—just the two of us, alone, enjoying the presence of each other? Somewhere along the drive, I would reach over and hold her left hand. In our conversations, we often reflected on the day's events or discussed plans for the next few days.

How is it that the presence of someone you love can create such a calm and peaceful atmosphere?

I guess it's the same way that her absence produces such a sense of aloneness. So, I did what I have done each time that sense overwhelms me. I prayed. I thanked God for the life Tootie and I had shared, thanked Him for His grace, and asked Him to give her a hug for me.

Yes, heaven is for real. But as much as I delight in knowing that she is with the Lord, my heart still aches. And how thankful I am that it does. The greater the love, the greater the heartache. And I loved her so much.

December 7, 2011: Teardrops

This year could be subtitled "Cry Me a River." I don't mind admitting that the tears have flowed—frequently. Sometimes my eyes just well up. Other times a trickle of a tear leaves a shiny path down my face. And there have been times lately when the tears are more like raindrops. I am talking about the kind that go "splash."

I'm not sure why now is any different from ten months ago, but I have noticed a difference.

Maybe it's because I have tended to ponder more. During my conversations with the Lord, I ponder the past, the present, and the future. I imagine that the Lord is sitting beside me, so I just have a conversation with Him. By doing so, I have found that the conversation flows easily. I can sense when my tears are building, but lately when they fall, they feel enormous. I can almost hear the splash-splash.

I must admit: my soul feels refreshed after having such a "conversation." I almost view these tears as a physical reflection of a spiritual soul-wash as the Lord renews my spirit.

Thank you, Lord, that I can be myself in your presence. Your comfort is more than a feeling. It's a moment of grace that overflows through my tears ducts. Amen.

December 10, 2011: A Concert

Daughter Taryn came to spend a couple of days with her dad! She stayed Friday and Saturday night, helped clean up a few things, baked me some cookies, and then suggested we drive to Duluth for a Christmas concert. Normally, I would have politely declined, but the idea of an evening of praise and worship songs sounded like a good tonic for my wounded soul. Besides, she said that the group—called "Shane and Shane"—were singing along with an artist named Phil Wickam. I had not heard of either of them, but Taryn said that any twenty-year-old would be impressed if a man of my age went to hear them. Regardless of the fact that I do not know any twenty-year-olds, the idea of being "cool," if only for a moment, was appealing.

The concert turned out to be worth the drive. Listening to great harmony and vocals encouraged and uplifted my spirit.

What is it about praise songs that stirs the soul and uplifts it?

Lord, thank you for the gift of children. I am blessed. Thank you for the gift of song. I stand amazed at the creative talents I heard tonight, all a reflection of Your image. I cling to You with my heart, my soul—and even my ears. Amen.

December 12, 2011: A Whiff

Cleaning out a drawer today, I discovered one of those small, travel-size perfume bottles. I instantly recognized it as one of Tootie's favorite scents.

The temptation was too great. I held it close and breathed in.

It was only a whiff, but it was enough to cause my knees to buckle, my stomach to tighten, and my eyes to go misty. All from a whiff. To say that memories flooded my soul is like saying Niagara Falls is a trickle. It's funny how such simple things trigger memories. I guess some folks might see such behavior as masochistic.

Not me. I cherish these moments. I don't linger too long or allow them to ruin my day. No, now such events become like a joyful walk down memory lane, a moment to ponder anew the blessing that my wife was to me and to cherish a thought, just as one savors the taste of a delicious delicacy—all from a whiff.

Lord, thank you for the sense of smell. I delight in how you made each one of us. Amen.

December 14, 2011: The Christmas Letter

Since the kids were in high school (the late 1980s), Tootie and I have sent out a Christmas letter in lieu of a card. It was usually an update on family happenings, accented with my special sense of humor. I struggled this year over whether I should—or even could—send out a letter. However, many people continue to ask, "How are you doing?"

Driving home from church a few weeks ago, I contemplated how I might articulate an answer to that question. Leaving the church parking lot, an idea started to take form. By the time I pulled into my garage, I knew what I wanted to do and immediately started to draft the letter. Here's the final version I mailed out today:

December 2011

Dear Family and Friends,

Merry Christmas to one and all. For the past thirty-eight years, Tootie and I have sent out Christmas greetings. For the past twenty-five years, we sent a Christmas letter conveying our Christmas wishes and bringing family and friends up to date with all the latest happenings of the McElhannon family. Christmas has always been the most joyful time of the year for our family.

This year is different.

Since losing Tootie to breast cancer this past January, I can truly say that 2011 has been the most difficult year of my life. Approaching this first Christmas without her is something I have yet to fully grasp or embrace. After all, it is the first season since Lyndon Johnson was President that I am not looking forward to giving the woman I love her Christmas presents. Yet as I reflect upon 2011, I realize that, for a time of such loneliness, I have never sensed God's presence more. And for a season of such heartache, I have never felt more loved by Him whose birth we celebrate. Yes, Christmas this year will be more than celebrating a birth. It will be a time to celebrate the gift of His presence and unconditional love.

This Spring, I found solace in chronicling Tootie's battle by writing a book called *Walking through the Valley of the Shadow*. It was a healing experience for me, and judging from the response from many of you, an inspirational read.

Our family rallied together and rejoiced in April, when daughter Maggie married Bryan Combs of Greensboro, Georgia. They also recently announced that they are expecting our first grandchild next February. Oh, happy day!

Most of the family was also able to join me in June for a family vacation in Maine, where we enjoyed lots of lobster, L.L.Bean, and time together as a family.

Thank you for your prayers and support this year. I wish I could give each of you a hug! But for now, allow me to simply wish you a Christmas filled with the blessings of love and family.

May the joy of the Lord be your strength in 2012!

Merry Christmas,
Buddy McElhannon
(buddymac@bellsouth.net)

On the back of the Christmas letter, I also included the following: "Friends, driving home from church a couple of weeks ago, I wondered if I could even write the annual Christmas letter this year. How could I explain my situation to so many of you who ask how things are going? The short story below is what I wrote when I got home. God bless."

The Great Musician's Birthday

As the Great Musician's birthday approached, the Pianist was unsure how he would handle the upcoming festivities. Musicians everywhere celebrated the Great Musician's birthday. They had come to know that playing his music, and his music alone, produced a sound that was far beyond any other. So too had the Pianist and his Partner always looked forward to this annual event.

After all, the Pianist and his Partner had played a duet for almost four decades. With each passing year, this duo had fine-tuned their performances. The longer they played together, the more they sounded as one, as each anticipated the sounds of the other. There was joyous harmony as each focused upon the direction of the Great Musician.

How they marveled at the music they made together. When they played, their melodious tunes made them both want to dance. Most marvelous was how much better they played when they followed the lead of the Great Musician. Oh, how they loved to play his music and how they cherished playing it together!

But the Pianist's Partner had been promoted to the Great Symphony. Now the Pianist played alone. Or so he tried. The sound was just not the same. The notes seemed dull, and it was hard to read the music through his tears. Was he out of tune or just out of touch? There was no longer any joy in his music. He had always relied on his Partner's consonant play for the reassurance that he was following the Great Musician's lead. But now the passion to play was gone.

The Pianist questioned the Great Musician. Why now? Why her? The Great Musician patiently listened and assured the Pianist that he too would be promoted sometime in the future. But for now, his song was not finished. He needed to continue to play. Sitting alone before his piano, the Pianist still found it hard to play even one note. The music just did not come—until the Great Musician sat down beside him, wiped away his tears, placed his hands upon those of the Pianist and began to play.

The sounds came softly at first. Soon, the Pianist realized that he was never really a solo act. The Great Musician had always delighted in playing his music through the heart and hands of the Pianist. And as the Pianist opened his heart to the Great Musician, his soul was flooded with a peace that defied description. Gradually, the music began to flow once again.

Maybe the Pianist would celebrate the birthday of the Great Musician after all.

Merry Christmas, everyone.

December 21, 2011: Rose Hill Again

The next few days will be busy. I decided to make my Christmas visit to the cemetery today. It's a Wednesday. I am off the rest of the week, and it seemed like a good time to go. It occurred to me that someone unfamiliar with grief might scoff at the idea of driving forty-five minutes to Winder, spending twenty minutes at a grave site, and driving forty-five minutes back. To those still in the waiting line for grief, my actions today may appear to be a waste of time. Oh, how wrong they would be.

While the frequency of my visits will likely change over time, this journey is more of a pilgrimage for me—a pilgrimage in the sense that it is a journey to a sacred place. While I fully realize that the spirit is now absent from the body (thanks be to God), this cemetery is still the place where my beloved's body—the body created in the image of God, the temple of the Holy Spirit—rests.

As such, this place is sacred ground.

My visits never last long. I place flowers on the graves of my grandmother, my mother, and my wife. I thank God for each of them and express through tears my humble gratefulness for the blessing Tootie was to me. This is not a duty, nor is it done out of some sense of obligation. I find it spiritually refreshing to come, say a prayer, shed some tears, and drive home reflecting on my life—past, present, and future. I am so grateful that my heart aches, not over regrets but over the loss of someone special, someone I loved until death did us part. My gratefulness comes from seeing too many lives and marriages shattered by regret, selfishness, and greed. Yes, I am thankful that my heartache is a good grief.

Lord, I once again give praise to You. I know that when Psalm 34 says to bless your name at all times, it means to bless your name at all times. And so I do so now. You are the Lord, and there is no other. My bride is now with you, and for that I am eternally grateful. Amen.

December 25, 2011: A Christmas to Remember

Frankly, I was not looking forward to the past two days—as if my mind, heart, and soul needed any reminder of what is lost. I expected Tootie's birthday (December 24) and Christmas Day to be the worst days of my life, other than January 28 earlier this year.

I must admit, however, that Maggie's suggestion to spend the weekend with her and Bryan in their home proved to be a wonderful idea. I arrived in the early afternoon of Friday, December 23. I unloaded a rather full car. Soon, Mari and Andrew, as well as Taryn and Algernon, arrived. I spent a leisurely day with three of the most beautiful women in the world. What father would not enjoy this day? On Saturday, Joel and Rosemary, along with Russ and Erin, arrived to complete the gathering of the immediate family. Of course, my brothers Jim and Andy, along with Andy's wife, Alma, also arrived to make the gathering truly complete.

I focused on cooking egg rolls: 140 of them. Bryan's family also arrived to enjoy this McElhannon Christmas specialty. Earl and Libby Combs, along with Doug and Lowell Combs and their two daughters, made for a full house of nineteen people. Then Tootie's mom and brothers Ronnie and Kevin arrived to increase the party to twenty-two people. Add in seven dogs, and let's just say that there was no time or place to feel sorry for oneself.

Later that afternoon, after the Combs had left, we gathered for the exchange of gifts. That evening, thirteen of us went to the nearby clubhouse for a buffet dinner. Finally, to cap a very busy Christmas Eve, a few of us attended midnight Mass.

Christmas morning found me frying up three pounds of bacon and a stack of pancakes before I passed out my gifts. By the time noon arrived, I found it hard to believe that the past forty-eight hours had passed so quickly. And the day was still not over.

Rosemary and Joel were having a late afternoon dinner with her parents, and they invited me to fry a turkey at their Athens home. I think she was afraid Joel might burn their new home down, and she welcomed an experienced turkey fryer like myself.

It was an enjoyable time spent with the Harbesons. By the time I arrived home around 8:00 p.m., I was truly exhausted, but in a good way. I took a long, hot shower and sat down to pray and praise God for a day spent with my family. Yes, Tootie's absence hung over me like a heavy weight around my neck. But I could see her in each of our children, and their presence made it easier to carry this burden. What a gift Tootie gave me in these five children! Even now, as adults, they still delight my heart and bring me joy.

Lord, I give thanks for the comfort You provide through the love and encouragement of friends and family. Amen.

Postscript: Since we all were spending this Christmas together, I decided to write my children a Christmas letter and place it in their stockings—just a love note from their dad.

Dear Joel, Russ, Taryn, Maggie, & Mari,

Over the years you have received Christmas notes from Santa, or in recent years, a letter from dear old Dad. You probably think you have long outgrown such sentimental expressions. Maybe so. But for obvious reasons, this year is different. So, for one more time, I wanted to express in written form my heartfelt wishes for each of you.

As I have pondered Christmases past, I must admit that, with few exceptions, I have long forgotten the gifts received. The memories I cherish are those of you and your mom, of Christmas Eve dinners followed by gift-giving and worship. Of course, Christmas mornings will never be the same either. At least I hope not. Please do not wait outside my bedroom door and whisper to one another, "Is it 7:00 a.m. yet? Can we wake Dad up?"

As I approached this Christmas season, I purposely kept the holiday shopping and decorating to a minimum. Yes, part of it was just a reflection of my grieving. But I also have to admit that, in finding the comfort that only God can provide, I am seeing Christmas in a whole new light. It has always been a joyful time as we celebrate the "Reason for the Season." But now I am aware as never before that the Reason for the Season is not Jesus. The Reason for the Season is not the *who* but the *why*. Jesus came to give light to "those who sit in darkness and the shadow of death" (Luke 1:79). Now "tidings of comfort and joy" means more than just a Christmas cliché.

Thank you for your love and support. I could not have made it through this year without you.

The greatest gift your mom ever gave me was the gift of the five of you. I will forever celebrate Christmas Eve as a day to honor her for her precious five gifts, and I will forever celebrate Christmas as a day that brought comfort to a hurting world and a wounded soul like me.

Come, let us adore Him.
Love ya, Dad

January 1, 2012: A New Year

Most folks would think I would welcome a new year. After all, 2011 was the year I lost Tootie, an entire year spent in grief. So yes, part of me welcomes 2012. Yet 2011 was a year of extraordinary change. Life will never be the same. I will never be the same.

Letting go, I have realized, is not so easy.

I discovered every holiday, birthday, and anniversary to be an emotional minefield. I might as well have pulled out a ball peen hammer and given myself a whack upside the head. There were times early in 2011 when that would have felt better than a heart-wrenching walk through memory lane. Yes, I am handling things better now, some eleven months later, but I am cautious, with each occasion, to walk carefully through the day. New Year's Eve was no exception.

December 31 was not unlike an anniversary date, birthday, or holiday. After three years of dating and thirty-eight-plus years of marriage, I know exactly where I was on every one of those dates.

I was with Tootie.

In the early years, we were usually at someone's party, ringing in the New Year. Later, it was not unusual for us to join friends in a prayer vigil, welcoming in the New Year with prayer and praise. More often in later years, we simply enjoyed the evenings by ourselves with a romantic dinner at home, listening to the fireworks in the distance, as if someone was celebrating our love for each other. Last year, December 31, 2010, was the most quiet one of all, as Tootie, her health deteriorating, retired early to bed.

This year, I was content to spend New Year's Eve alone, cleaning house, starting my latest writing project, and catching a Bowl game or two. But yet again, this day would be one where I felt the warmth, encouragement, and love of family and friends.

It started with my usual Saturday morning walk with John Kommeth. This particular December morning was rather brisk but still comfortable enough, even at 8:00 a.m., for a five-mile walk. Followed by refreshments at a nearby Chick-fil-A, this time of exercise and fellowship continues to be a welcome exercise of body and spirit. I expected the rest of the day to be a quiet one.

I received a belated Christmas card from a friend who expressed his love, prayers, and support. Some of the kids called to check and see how things were going. Taryn invited me down for dinner, but I opted out, not wanting to spend any time traveling on this day. I did decide to attend our 5:00 p.m. vigil Mass. It was not only a spiritually refreshing worship experience, but I saw many friends, including my pastor, Father John, who came over to hug me and offer encouragement. I returned home to find a neighbor waiting to drop off some food, and then I received a call from my cousin JoJo, who just wanted to let me know that he and Debbie were thinking of me and praying for me.

So, as midnight approached, and with the sound of firecrackers in the distance, I sat down for my evening devotional. Grateful for the blessings of family and friends, I quietly prayed in the New Year—alone.

Once again, I sought the Lord's blessing upon my growing prayer list of family and friends and those God had placed upon my heart. Somehow, having my "quiet" time amidst the cacophony of neighborhood fireworks seemed to be a metaphor for my life this year: a quiet faith on the inside while chaos seemed to rule outside.

To my surprise, I slept for eight and a half hours, the longest I have slept in eighteen months. The year 2012 is finally here.

Oh, Lord, as each passing holiday and anniversary is a reminder of my loss, so too is each one a reminder of your love for me. You are indeed near to the brokenhearted. You are my balm of Gilead. Your healing touch is never more present then during these times of heartache.

He heals the brokenhearted and binds up their wounds.
—Psalm 147:3

January 7, 2012: Planning to Give

In recent years, Tootie and I made it a practice to take the first week of January to outline our personal financial plan for the coming year. Years ago we did a year-end analysis and were disappointed in our management of the financial blessings God had bestowed. We purposed to give more forethought to our giving strategy for the year ahead.

More than merely making an annual budget, we prayed and agreed on what ministries would receive our tithe. Our local church received 5 percent, and the remaining 5 percent was allocated to the ministries the Lord placed upon our hearts.

The last time we did this together was January 2010. Last year, she had been too sick, so I continued our 2010 plan into 2011. Now, as I plan my 2012 giving, I realize how much we depended on each other to check and balance our direction. It was such a joy to agree together on whom we would bless the coming year. I miss her heart of gratitude, her generous spirit, and her encouragement to always be looking for someone in need of a helping hand.

Thank you, Lord, for the gift of Your Son. I pray, even as Your grace is poured out upon me, that I may simply be a channel of blessing to others. Amen.

Give, and it will be given to you; good measure,
pressed down, shaken together, running over, they
will pour into your lap. For by your standard of
measure it will be measured to you in return.
—Luke 6:38

January 9, 2012: The Gauntlet Continues

Halfway. I am over halfway through a sixty-day gauntlet. At least that is what it feels like. It started with Thanksgiving, followed by Tootie's birthday (December 24), Christmas, and now January. The next few weeks hold a flood of memories, mostly bad ones.

It was one year ago today that I woke up at 4:00 a.m. Tootie was throwing up blood. Soon we were in Rockdale Hospital's ER. Things went downhill from there.

I am still taking one day at a time. I can't ignore these feelings, these memories. Staying busy helps, but who am I kidding? Distractions never last long enough; the memories simply wait for an opportune moment to crash into my thoughts. I have accepted that this crescendo of emotions will come, regardless of what I do. I will roll with the flow and find a way to get through the end of the month. Maggie's baby is due soon: the one bright light to an otherwise dismal month.

I talked with one of my colleagues today. I explained that 2011 has been like walking in a fog, a fog so thick that it's all I can do to take one day at a time. As the year progressed, the fog lifted slightly but never enough to see very far down the road. My tomorrows are hidden by this lingering cloud. Time doesn't heal. It simply allows the fog to lift ever so slowly.

Lord, You indeed are a lamp unto my feet. Maybe I should have been walking one day, one step at a time, anyway. Thank you for guiding my steps. Amen.

Thy word is a lamp to my feet and a light to my path.
—Psalm 119:105

And I will lead the blind by a way they do not
know, in paths they do not know I will guide them.
I will make darkness into light before them and
rugged places into plains. These are the things
I will do, and I will not leave them undone.
—Isaiah 42:16

January 10, 2012: A Frosted Orange

I left work a little early today. I had a hard time concentrating. Today is the forty-third anniversary of our first date. I kept flashing back to 1969, remembering the night that changed my life.

How could I have known on that cold January evening that there would never be anyone else?

Unfortunately, I also kept flashing back to January 10, 2011. A snowstorm had hit Atlanta, Tootie was in ICU at Rockdale Hospital, and I was still reeling from the gastroenterologist's report about Tootie's stomach. In between those two January tenths was a lifetime of love and marriage. Little did I know that she only had eighteen days to live.

As I left work today, I drove by an Atlanta landmark, the world's largest drive-in restaurant: The Varsity. It was here on January 10, 1969, that we came for a late-night snack after watching the movie *Funny Girl* at the Capri Theater in Buckhead. Tootie ordered her favorite, a "frosted orange." I was tempted to stop there today and do the same, but good judgment prevailed. I am not sure I could have drunk it, much less kept it down. I prefer to have only good memories of a Varsity's frosted orange.

Lord, how many times can I say thank you? How many times can I lift my hands, bow my head, and pour out my heart and say, "Praise You, Lord, for the gift of a loving wife." I am humbled even now by the blessing Tootie was for me and the cherished memories that flow from just the thought of a frosted orange. Amen.

January 17, 2012: Nanny's Heart Attack

January is becoming a month of sorrows. I got word today that Tootie's mom, Zelma Smith, had a serious heart attack. She's ninety-three. Initial reports are not good. The impending birth of Maggie and Bryan's baby seems to be the only redeeming event in January.

Lord, I ask your blessing upon our family, as another loss appears to be imminent. Amen.

January 19, 2012: A Dessert for Refuge

First, news from Eatonton is good. Zelma responded to medication and seems to have survived this initial attack. Amazingly, they are talking about releasing her in the next couple of days. No surgery is planned. The doctor doesn't think she could survive it at age ninety-three. I pray that another attack won't happen soon.

Tonight, Refuge Pregnancy Center held a fund-raising dessert reception at Rockdale Community Church. With the good news about Zelma, I relaxed and attended the event. Good music and wickedly delicious desserts abounded. It was good to see several friends who attend RCC, as well as the ladies of Refuge. Tootie loved this kind of thing. I don't think it raises much money, but good fellowship is always sweet—as are the desserts. Yet attending is a mixed blessing. I certainly enjoy seeing folks, but the awareness of Tootie's absence is never more acute than at events like this. Nevertheless, I go.

The comfort of friends outweighs the heartache.

Lord, thank you for the encouragement I received tonight. It's almost a year later, and still believers who knew Tootie offer words of encouragement to me. Thanks be to You, God. Amen.

Therefore encourage one another and build up
one another, just as you also are doing.
—1 Thessalonians 5:11

January 26, 2012: A Kiss from God

Leaving work today, I turned on the radio to one of the local Christian stations. I caught the beginning of a message from one of my favorite Christian ministers, Mark Rutland. Mark is a former Methodist turned Assemblies-of-God preacher. He is also president of Oral Roberts University. I have heard him in person several times, but the time I most remember is when he and his wife conducted a marriage seminar in the mid-eighties at a hotel in Madison, Georgia. Tootie and I attended, and it was a transformational event. The dude can preach. And when I hear his voice, I have many fond memories of a 1980s weekend in Madison, Georgia.

Today his message was on Psalm 112, which opens with "Praise the LORD! How blessed is the man who fears the LORD, who greatly delights in His commandments." It was a message of encouragement and brought comfort to my spirit.

Then, later this evening I read my daily email post from Ravi Zacharias ministries (*SLICE*, January 26, 2012). This one was titled "Dark Though It Is." Well, the title certainly rings true, but one particular quote by Anne Lamott caught my eye: "Man is born broken … He lives by mending. The grace of God is glue."

Actually, it's more like superglue. It is yet another reminder of how God comforts the brokenhearted.

At evening's end, I picked up my devotional, *Jesus Calling*, and the words for January 26 jumped off the page and echoed through every corner of my heart and mind: "It is possible to enjoy Me and glorify Me in the midst of adverse circumstances. In fact, My Light shines most brightly through believers who trust Me in the dark … I am much less interested in right circumstances than in right responses to whatever comes your way." And the verses of the day? Psalm 112:4 and 7. I had to smile. I had just received a heavenly kiss. Through a radio program, an email, and a few words in a book, the God of eternity took a moment in time to comfort this broken soul. My mending continues.

Thank you, Lord, for being a God of comfort.

> Blessed are those who mourn, for
> they shall be comforted.
> —Matthew 5:4

January 28, 2012: One Year

Today is the one-year anniversary of Tootie's death. This date had been looming on my calendar, as I anticipated it being an emotionally charged weekend. Two days ago, I received an email from a dear friend who lost an adult daughter a decade ago. She expressed her thoughts and prayers for my family and offered encouragement for this weekend. One insight she offered was that the anticipation of the one-year anniversary was far worse than the actual day itself. I had to agree. Somehow I had created within my mind this image of January 28, 2012, as a day of lamentation followed by the sound of a trumpet and a shout from heaven, formally announcing, "Okay. Grieving time is now concluded." Yeah, right. Reality is that grieving does not somehow evaporate after a year.

Is it still painful? Yes. Is it still ever present? Yes.

My friend also suggested that I make plans for the day but be flexible. So my plans were simple. Make a visit to the cemetery, lay some flowers on Tootie's grave, say my prayers, and have a conversation with her one more time. Fortunately, Maggie, Bryan, and Taryn were also able to join me. I was tempted to make this a solo visit, but if I am honest, I must say that it was good to have company. My children are an everlasting reminder of the love Tootie and I shared. Their presence is always a welcome comfort.

Maggie's baby is due any day now. I had to laugh when she got out of the car and waddled over to Taryn and me. Taryn placed her hands upon Maggie's stomach, leaned over as if to converse with baby Combs, and said, "It's okay to come out now. We have chocolate out here!" Seeing no visible response, I can draw only one conclusion: it must be a boy. Some comic relief was welcome.

After a lunch together, Maggie and Bryan headed home to Greensboro, and Taryn and I headed to Conyers. A short stop at an antique mall in Monroe turned into three stops. Ninety minutes later, we emerged, impressed with how Monroe was becoming a mecca of antique stores.

This was a nostalgic stop for me. In the summer of 2010, Tootie and I had visited the same shops. Walking through them today with Taryn brought back a wave of sweet memories. Such reflections no longer result in stomach cramps. Oh, there may be a tear or two, but now cherishing such memories is more like a good soak in a hot tub. I can close my eyes and remember the smile on her face when she found "it." I no longer remember all of the "its" she found, but I'll never forget that smile. That was the true treasure.

Lord, for a beautiful day and for the comfort of family, I humbly thank you. I seem to taste Your blessings with each new day, and my heart savors the peace that only comes from You. Amen.

Be anxious for nothing, but in everything by prayer
and supplication with thanksgiving let your requests
be made known to God. And the peace of God,
which surpasses all comprehension, shall guard
your hearts and your minds in Christ Jesus.
—Philippians 4:6–7

January 31, 2012: The Answers Will Have to Wait

Over a year has passed, and I still have questions that have not been answered. Most of these questions begin with the word *why*. I know—yes, I know—that short of heaven I will never have those answers. It is becoming ever clearer that this year has been a battle for my heart and soul. If I allow my heart and mind to be obsessed with all of the "don't knows," then I am simply greasing the path to despair. I must cling to that which is certain.

Recently I read that you should never trade what you do know for what you don't know. That makes so much sense to me. I may still be a grieving husband, but I do believe in the truths of Scripture and the promises of God.

I know there is a God.

I know God loves me.

I know God yearns to have a relationship with me.

I know that serving the Lord does not mean you will avoid trials or suffering.

I know it is appointed once for us to die.

I know that God brings good out of suffering, even though we cannot always see it.

I know, according to God's Word, that following death, the Christian enters into the presence of God.

I know that my beloved Tootie had a personal relationship with Jesus Christ, and at this very moment she is enjoying the fellowship of God and all those who have gone before. This is not because she was a good wife (which she was) or a good mother (which she was) or a good person (she was that too). It is because she made a commitment to embrace her faith, embrace her Lord, accept His death as a sacrifice for her sins, and seek to grow in fellowship with the risen Lord. Heaven is not a reward for her good deeds. It is simply a continuation of the relationship she already had. She is home.

Lord, how grateful I am that, of all the unanswered questions, You are not one of them.

In my trouble, I cried to the LORD,
and He answered me.
—Psalm 120:1

February 3, 2012: The Mystery of Grace

The doctor told Maggie to be patient. She is three days past her due date. She plans another visit to the doctor on Monday. I am still in awe of this baby's arrival so close on the heels of the anniversary of Tootie's death. Coincidence?

Call it what you will, I call it the goodness of God.

I came across another quote today by novelist Anne Lamott that made me sit up and say, "Amen." The quote so perfectly captures the wonder of it all: "I do not understand the mystery of grace—only that it meets us where we are and does not leave us where it found us." The more I ponder this mystery, the more I want to fall upon my knees and thank God for such an undeserved gift.

Lord, I don't understand it, but I humbly accept the grace You have poured out upon me. I do not deserve it, but I undeniably need it for true healing. Amen.

> O LORD my God, I cried to Thee for
> help and Thou didst heal me.
> —Psalm 30:2

February 4, 2012: A Year to Remember

I started this journal one year ago today. Yes, 2011 has been a year like no other.

- I discovered loneliness.
- I discovered heartache.

- I discovered the pain of separation from the one person I loved more than life itself.
- I discovered that the human capacity for tears has no limits.
- I discovered grief. Rather, grief found me, because I certainly did not go looking for it.

Grief has been a selfish, demanding companion. Shouting for attention, like the world's worst toothache, it refuses to be ignored and seeks to fill every moment. But I also discovered along the way that good grief brings healing and peace, that family and friends are true treasures, and that the Lord has borne my griefs and carried my sorrows (Isaiah 53:4). He is a God of comfort.

Lord, what else can I say but thank you for being a God who is always there—in my darkest hour and my deepest need.

The eternal God is a dwelling place, and
underneath are the everlasting arms.
—Deuteronomy 33:27

February 11, 2012: A Day of Tears

The tears flowed today. But unlike any time in the past year, these tears were not the response to a broken heart, to a lost love, or to grief uncontrolled. No, today the tears came from eyes that beheld the gift of life, from a grateful heart belonging to a new grandfather. These tears were more like a gulp of cold water to a parched tongue. These tears were tears of joy.

My first grandchild was born today. Alden Douglas Combs entered this world around 2:00 p.m., and for the first time in a year, my heart sang.

I started this journal over a year ago. Today, I bring it to a close. A year ago, my heart was overwhelmed with grief, saturated with a sense of loss that saw no end to this valley of tears. I could not see how life could continue. I may have been standing in the palm of God's hand, but life was so shrouded by the fog of grief that I could not see the heavenly hands that held me so close.

Now the fog has begun to lift.

Yes, memories of Tootie will be cherished forever, and my tears of heartache will always be a reminder of a *we* that became an *I*. Yet my grandson's birth has been like a chorus of trumpets sounding forth that life is sacred and God's love and grace will always be there.

My son-in-law held his new son in his arms. His tears flowed out of a joy and love beyond description. As I drove home from the hospital, contemplating the joyful events of the day, I realized that my heavenly Father, in much the same way, has been holding me close. The holy Comforter brought comfort to my wounded heart. My tears were only exceeded by those of the Man of Sorrows. Yes, I know that God is near the brokenhearted, because His grace has restored my soul.

May I bless His name forever.

Lord, thank you for your faithfulness and love beyond measure. I realize now that this past year has been but one long prayer. The first stanza of the hymn, "Be Thou Near to Me," sums it up so simply:

Oh, Lord I come with heart, here open, For in my
hour of darkness I may be Seeking the joy of love
unspoken Oh, Lord, be Thou near to me.

*Lord, You are a God of truth and compassion. Today has been a
joyful reminder that You are the Lord, and there is no other. Amen.
Amen. Amen.*

Final Words

Ecclesiastes 3:1 opens with: "There is an appointed time for everything." It speaks of a time to weep and a time to mourn. I must confess that even after a year, I find it hard to completely or easily move out of this season of mourning. I am keenly aware of how dynamic the grief process is. Such a loss precludes any return to the way things used to be. Such a loss, I have discovered, would either destroy me or change me forever. Apart from the grace of God, despair is like a black hole that sucks you in. Being thankful for what I had rather than being consumed by what I have lost is the only way I found to avoid despair's magnetic appeal.

The waves of grief still billow, but now they are overcome by an ocean of faithfulness—God's faithfulness. "Great Is Thy Faithfulness" is more than just a hymn. It is a song of praise, a recognition that God's promises do not fail.

This past year, with each passing day, I discovered anew that "Thou changest not, Thy compassions, they fail not."

And with each new sunrise, I learned that "morning by morning, new mercies I see."

And I was able to proclaim, "Great is Thy faithfulness, Lord, unto me!"

Lord, for reasons unknown, Tootie took the early train home. I remain. My prayer is that, like Tootie, I finish well. May the words of my mouth, the meditations of my heart, and all that I do be pleasing in Your sight. Thank you, Lord, for carrying my sorrows, for bearing my grief and walking with me through this valley of tears.

About the Author

In late September 2010, Buddy McElhannon and his wife, Mary—known to family and friends as Tootie—discovered she had breast cancer. Diagnosed as an aggressive form of stage two cancer, they nevertheless expected a long battle. It proved to be a short one. Tootie passed away just four months later on January 28, 2011.

With his thirty-eight year marriage brought to a sudden end by this evil disease, Buddy now found himself alone at the age of fifty-nine, overwhelmed with grief, confusion, and more questions than answers. Seeking a way to express all of the turmoil within, he began to journal his feelings, his questions, and his prayers. Walking through the Valley of Tears is an intimate look into one man's journey through grief. Part devotional, part confessional, Buddy's journal provides a transparent view into how one man not only survived his personal valley of tears but emerged with a stronger faith in the God who comforts the broken hearted.

Buddy McElhannon is a 41 year employee with AT&T. He married his high school sweetheart, Tootie, in 1972. He and Tootie had five children. He now lives in Conyers, Georgia.

32354545R00076

Made in the USA
Lexington, KY
17 May 2014